Debbie Scott

52 MORE PROGRAMS THAT POP

A year of fun programing for Senior Adults in Nursing
Homes, Adult Day Centers and Churches group.

"52 More Programs That Pop, A Year of Fun Programming for Senior Adults in Nursing Homes, Adult Daycare, and in Church Groups" by Debbie Ann Scott ISBN 978-1-951985-92-9 (softcover).

FOREWORD

I have had the privilege of working with senior adults in churches, adult daycare centers, nursing homes, assisted living facilities, and in community groups. Their wisdom, experience, love of life, and sense of humor are to be treasured, honored, and imitated. May the activities contained in this book inspire smiles, laughter, thought, and health. In the process, may community be built and love be shared.

Special thanks to my son the graphic designer for my cover. You can see more of his work at www.BeardedBeeDesign.com.

Contents

JANUARY

Fruitcake Day

Food:

- Fruitcake, panettone or stollen, Eggnog, coffee, tea, panettone cake, or raisin cake

Craft:

- Make fruitcakes
- Make ornaments of holiday favorite shapes from clay. Paint another day or mold clay ahead of time with group to paint this day. Ornaments can be heart shaped to use for Valentine's Day decorations.

History:

Fruitcake is one of the traditions at Christmas time that brings a debate by many people, either you like fruitcake, or you hate it. The late-night host Johnny Carson's joked; there was only one fruitcake in the world that people keep re-gifting. This candied fruit and nuts cake has a history beginning in the Middle ages.

Many different recipes combine candied fruits, nuts, & spices, mixed with butter, eggs and flour, into a dense cake to serve during the holiday seasons. Some like to soak their fruitcakes in rum, while others prefer to eat it without the alcohol soak. Some Egyptians had an interesting tradition with a fruitcake. You would be surprised to see a fruitcake in the tomb of a loved one for the deceased to enjoy in the afterlife.

Holiday fruitcakes were popular items to send soldiers at war, so they would have a little bit of Christmas while they were away from home. Fruitcakes did not spoil without refrigeration as the soldiers were in battle or camping at war. One soldier forgot about receiving the cake, as he returned home from war and accidentally packed away with his service items. Forty years later, he found the fruitcake. Although he did not eat the 40-year-old fruitcake, it appeared to be fine and not spoiled.

Many different countries have holiday cakes like fruitcake. In Germany, a similar cake is called stollen and in Italy, the cake with fruit is panettone. Both cakes use similar ingredients, but they are lighter and less dense than fruitcake enjoyed at holidays. In Australia, India, and Bulgaria you can find fruitcakes all year around because it is a treat eaten throughout the year. In the Bahamas, rum is a major part of enjoying a piece of fruitcake. The ingredients are soaked 2 weeks to 3 months prior to the baking of the cakes in rum, as well as more rum pored over the hot, fresh cakes fresh from the oven.

In North America, unlike in many areas of the world, fruitcakes are a holiday treat and are rarely seen at other times during the year.

I guess the late-night host Johnny Carson was wrong. People from countries worldwide seem to enjoy fruitcake of some kind. They can't all be wrong. Why not shop for all the fruitcake ingredients, fire up the oven and give this taste treat a try.

Activities:

- Fruitcake word search puzzle..

- Make Bingo cards with ingredients on the cards. Ingredients include: candied fruit, nuts, butter, flour, raisins, coconut, vanilla extract, eggs, rum, and sugar. Put the different ingredients in a hat to draw out. Mini fruitcakes can be the prizes.

Fruitcake Ingredients Puzzle

```
W T S G G E Z R C F B I E G R
U U S U F S T F Q N L M Y E X
O N E D S F R U I T T O T S E
X O L Y E N R L M O E T U K H
C C F A L L I N A V U G U R B
Y O R G Y R B S C B A I S Q R
F C I G A Z K A I R P E B Q T
U G S A U B N S J A H P C H Q
J R I C A D L X T C R Z Z P Q
S D N F I Q E I P U L O X Z B
S W G E F C M M G I N K X I L
K F D P D C O Z W A L B Q S P
I U P A E L N M E N B Y C B X
I P R P R J E D F Q E Y S S J
F N K Y S P U I M U C C C I H
```

BUTTER   CANDIED   COCONUT
EGGS   FLOUR   FRUIT
LEMON   NUTS   RAISINS
SELFRISING   SUGAR   VANILLA

National Bird Day

Food:
- Chicken nuggets, egg salad, deviled eggs, eggs for breakfast

Crafts:
- Cut bird bodies out of cardboard. Wrap the cardboard in yarn of your color choice. Use feathers to make the wings and hang with yarn from the middle of the bird body. Use a bird clipart outline for pattern.
- Use clay to mold birds. Make the birds ahead of time so they will be dry to paint, or you can mold the birds this day and paint them another day for a craft.
- Find outline clipart of birds to paint with watercolor paints.

History:

A favorite pastime for 50 million Americans is taking trips with a pair of binoculars into wooded areas to go bird watching. Retirees used bird watching as a fun pass time, slowing down and enjoying the outdoors after their busy career lifestyles. Seasoned bird watchers use guidebooks, binoculars and a handwritten notebook with bird photos with information about each bird observed. Older bird watchers leave their cell phone and worries behind, and take notes of what they actually observe during their bird watching adventures.

As people of all ages got interested in the hobby of bird watching, its name changed to "Birding." Cellphones technology, birding apps and digital cameras were used on birding trips. Seasoned birdwatchers felt that this technology was cheating the traditional activity of bird watching. And as this hobby has grown, a World Series of Birding event occurs every May. The American Birding Association has a code of ethics revising the use of the new technologies prohibited for serious bird watching competitions.

Birding has several reasons for growing in popularity, the main reason it is relatively inexpensive once you have your digital camera. You also can see birds everywhere you are, even in your back yard. It is a good outside activity with your families with younger children and it is challenging for the observers, and interesting learning about each bird. As your looking for birds, it develops focus and concentration for younger birding students. This trip into nature is relaxing, keeps you active and make you happy when you find new birds to record.

Some tips to locate birds is looking for colors in the trees, listening to their calls, and being patient while you bird watch. The sightings are difficult until you get the hang of it but becomes quite rewarding as your skills in observing increases. Looking for nests, migration patterns, and observing the trees before leaves cover the branches helps one to know where to locate the birds in the trees.

Another fun way to views easily is to have different types of bird feeders in your backyard. This will help you know what to look for as you venture out into the parks and trails. You may need to look up locations of nests for the different types of birds that you might want to see outside of a zoo environment. For example, eagle nests are usually quite large and are found in the tops of tall trees. Tips like these will make bird watching a successful adventure for all.

For more information, visit 15 fun facts about birds - https://www.mentalfloss.com/article/78996/15-amazing-facts-about-15-birds

Activities:

- Get bird sounds off the Internet and see if they can identify the bird.
- Birds around the world word search.
- Fun facts of birds to discuss.
- Bird Bingo. Make cards at this site below: https://wordmint.com/pages/landing/bingo?headline=Bingo+Card+Creator&_puzzle_type=Bingo&bing_loc_physical_ms=87097&msclkid=e66a508918cf185758070f5369f26955&utm_source=bing&utm_medium=cpc&utm_campaign=bing.wordmint.bingo.phrase&utm_term=create%20your%20own%20bingo&utm_content=phrase.bingo_creator

BIRDS AROUND THE WORLD

```
H C F H C Z F D I Y G L N B K
A U A S A J U I K C L U L H C
Y W M X R R C N N U H U J Q O
K J T M D H E U G C E J X A C
J N Y N I H E A R B H Y P C A
I A M L N N E E I O W Q H L E
A W K X A S G R D N Z U X I P
H S Q T L S D B X A C J V U C
U L E E S S D R I B K C A L B
D I A J H U Y C Q R I C Q G S
P I G E O N O W A J D W I I T
X L L D X C C T K P X S W H Y
P G E X T T J D N F S Z R F C
X L W O K R K S W Y C M D P E
R R T M R E Z P W G C P A L X
```

BLACKBIRD	BLUEBIRDS	CARDINALS
CHICKADEE	EAGLE	FINCH
HAWK	HUMMINGBIRDS	OWL
PEACOCK	PIGEON	SEAGULL

Kazoo Day

Food:

- Vegetable tray, finger sandwiches, cookies, cupcakes, muffins, or banana bread, any food item that is long and skinny like a Kazoo.

Crafts:

- Make hats to wear for your kazoo group. You can add feathers, rickrack, ribbons and buttons (anything that would make them fun.)

- Make a program schedule to hand out for a kazoo program.

History:

In 1840, two men created a fun little musical instrument. The first, an African American inventor, Alabama Vest and his partner Thaddeus Von Clegg, a German American clock maker. A small music instrument easily carried with you called a Kazoo. Another plus for this instrument is that anyone can play it, all you need to know how to do is hum. The introduction of the Kazoo was in 1852, at the Georgia State Fair as the "Down South Submarine." The kazoo really took off in 1912 when Emil Song commercially produced it in Western New York. Song joined a tool and die maker from Buffalo, New York, Michael McIntyre who moved this production of kazoos to Eden, New York. You can stroll through the factory museum to learn the history of the creating and making the kazoo.

Kazoo players have a debate on who really created the first kazoo. The Kaminsky International Kazoo Quartet argues that they were the first kazoo group, not Alabama Vest. Another toy maker, Simon Seller, in 1879 received a patent for a toy trumpet that works with this same principal as the kazoo. This toy trumpet as well as the kazoo, works on air pressure oscillating over a vibrating membrane. The player does not blow into the instrument, rather the musician hums into the kazoo making a unique vibrating sounding music.

A European conductor, David Bedford, joined 100 kazoo players to form a kazoo classical music group. His group does not have professional player, he simply hands out 100 kazoos to the audience and together with an instrumental ensemble created, and all enjoy an evening of music. What an enjoyable experience Bedford gives to all those who attend the evening of music and fun.

The Mills Brothers vocal group leads another European group. They started as a vaudeville type quartet and later added the kazoos. The unique feature of this quartet is that the group of kazoos players play in four-part harmony and the fifth brother accompanies them on his guitar. Another fun evening for the audience to enjoy.

No matter who invented the kazoo we all would agree, playing the kazoo is fun, easy, and enjoyed by people of all ages.

Activities:

- Play your favorite songs on Kazoos.

- Perform a program for families or staff. You could have group songs and solo songs. You can mix readings or poems among the kazoo songs.

National Bubble Wrap Day

Food:
- Rice Crispy Treats. (they are known for snap, crackle, and pop like the bubble wrap)
- Cottage cheese with canned fruit (peaches, pineapples).

Crafts:
- Use bubble wrap to cut out a beehive shape. With tempera paint, paint the bubble wrap yellow and let it dry. Get a blue piece of paper and draw a tree trunk and one limb to hold the beehive. Cut some green leaves or use scrunch green tissue paper for leaves. When the beehive is dry, glue the hive onto the limb. Around the hive puts some bees. How you make the bees is to use your index finger and dip it in yellow paint to make the body of the bees. For the wings dip your pinky into white paint and add two wings to each yellow fingerprint. When the bees are dry, paint black stripes on their body. (See patterns below on this page)
- Use bubble wrap to cut into a shape of a pineapple. Paint the bubble wrap yellow. While the bubble wrap is drying, cut out thin triangular leave in green for the top of the pineapple. Place the green leaves on the top of the bubble wrap for the top of the pineapples. Get a variety of foam core board colors for participants to choose, glue the bubble wrap pineapple onto the board, add the green triangle leaves. Underneath or above the pineapple, leave room for the words "Welcome" and/or your last name. (See patterns at bottom of the page)

History:
Alfred Fielding and Marc Chavannes, two Swiss engineers, accidentally discovered a fun plastic paper known as bubble wrap in 1957. These two, Hawthorne, New Jersey men, were trying to create a washable plastic wallpaper. They started by gluing two plastic shower curtains together, but the project did not come out smooth, instead it came out with many bubbles between the two shower curtains. The men thought they could pass their invention off as wallpaper, but it never took off.

Alfred's young son Howard, was very excited about his father's fun invention. The five-year-old son was excited when he discovered how much fun his father's invention was to play with. In fact, he was the first to pop the bubbles between the plastic layers, something we all enjoy and cannot seem to resist. Popping bubble wrap can be fun and can help reduce stress whenever needed.

This bumpy, funny feeling plastic is an excellent layer of protection when packing glass dishes or mailing a fragile item to a friend. All packing companies use bubble wrap when you bring items into ship around the world.

Bubble Wrap has many uses other than mailing packages for safe delivery. If your home is cold in the winter, using bubble wrap over your windows adds a barrier from the cold air getting in, creating an insulation for your home. You can also put bubble wrap in you outlets and light switches to prevent the cold air from leaking in around the fixtures and outlets. The switch plate covers up the bubble wrap, hiding your bubble wrap insulation. If you have a toilet that sweats when the temperature in the bathroom is warm, bubble wrap can be a good remedy. Just by lining the inside of the toilet with bubble wrap. To do this, you turn off your toilet water, flush the water out and dry the inside of the toilet. When dry, use a waterproof glue and adhere the bubble wrap on the inside of the toilet tank. When the bubble wrap glue is dry, turn back on the water and the toilet will not sweat due to the difference in temperature inside and outside the toilet tank.

Some use a piece of bubble wrap across their car windshield in the winter to keep your windshield protected and allow for easy clearing off the snow from the windshield. Others use some bubble wrap to prevent the door from hitting the wall when someone opens the door too wide, causing damage to either the door or wall. Men use bubble wrap in their toolbox to keep their tools from sliding around while traveling and damaging their tools. In addition, you might see bubble wrap in the vegetable draws in the refrigerator to keep the fruits and vegetables from getting bruised or spoiling. Then when the bubble wrap gets dirty, you simply remove the bubble wrap and replace it with a fresh new piece.

Gardeners can use bubble wrap too. Some use the wrap to put around their tools handles to help with the grip. Other put bubble wrap around the base of the strawberry plant to catch falling strawberries. This keeps the strawberries from bruising or rotting when they sit in the dirt. Wrapping the base of a plant can help keep moisture in the plants, creating a greenhouse effect. Bubble wrap around plants in your garden helps your new saplings get a good start, as well as keep the deer away. When the deer step on, or bite the bubble wrap, the popping spooks them and they run away. Bubble wrap can help gardeners protect their knees while kneeling to plant new plants or weed the garden beds. While kneeling to plant flowers and vegetables the bubble wrap creates a cushion between their knees and the ground. Finally, a piece of bubble wrap to cover your compost pile would create the perfect condition to promote decomposition.

Camping enthusiasts find that bubble wrap helps them to stay warm while camping, when used in their sleeping bags. Another layer of bubble wrap under your sleeping bag helps to cushion your body from the hard ground. A little problem might be the popping sound the bubble wrap makes when you move during the night and the noise wakes you up. To keep camping food fresh, bubble wrap can be the insulation needed to keep food from spoiling.

Cold weather sports participants may enjoy a layer of bubble wrap inside mittens to insulate hands from the cold. In case of an injury, use bubble wrap to keep the injury immobile until medical help arrives.

Some may use bubble wrap in their closet. When storing boots or purses when not in use, bubble wrap can keep the boots and purses in shape. Others may use bubble wrap to roll up their long hair if they want curls. Start at the bottom of your hair with a small strips of bubble wrap and roll the hair on the strips, when you get to your head, just tie the ends of the bubble wrap together. The great thing about using bubble wrap hair rollers is it creates a comfortable cushion for your head instead of lying on a hard rollers. In the morning you will have beautiful curls for the day.

Crafters can use bubble wrap for a variety of craft ideas. Use the small bubbles wrap, cut out a pineapple shape, and paint it yellow. Glue it onto a piece of paper or cardboard to make a welcome sign with a pineapple decoration. Use green paper for the green top of the pineapple. Alternatively, cut out a beehive shape and paint it yellow. (See craft ideas above). While the paint is drying, cut out a tree limb out of brown paper and glue it to the paper. Use green tissue paper for leaves on the tree. Next, take your finger and dip in yellow paint to make bee bodies. Then dip your finger into white paint for the wings. When it dries, use a fine black Sharpie to draw stripes on the bees. Another project with bubble wrap is to use a piece of bubble wrap as a stamp. Dip the bubble wrap in paint and create a fun design, by pressing it on paper. Finally, you can use the bubble wrap and other textured items to use to make different rubbings. Placer a piece of paper and taking a pencil or chalk and rubbing over the top of the textured items to create a fun design. You could lay a piece of bubble wrap on the table to dry Easter eggs on after dying them. The raised bubbles will allow air to get to all sides, making them dry faster.

The final creation might be for safety measures. If you fall a lot, you might want to think about having a suit of clothes and hat made of bubble wrap, to help cushion you from any future falls. SMILE!

Activities:
- Hand out a piece of bubble wrap and let each person pop a piece of bubble wrap.
- Divide the group into teams. Get one person in each group to volunteer to wrap in bubble wrap. The other members take a roll or two of bubble wrap and see who could wrap their team member in bubble wrap first.
- Divide group in teams or work as one group to think of new ways to use bubble wrap.

BEE HIVE

PINEAPPLE

The Creation of the Yo-Yo

Food:
- Round Cookies, pumpkin roll, or use Ding-Dongs cupcakes, and cut them in half letting the cream filling circular design show. Coffee, tea or milk.

Craft:
- Color the sides of yo-yos. You can find craft yo-yos at hobby store for purchase. You will need permanent markers to color the designs on the sides of the yo-yos, so that the color will not bleed off on your hands when you use the yo-yos.
- Make a "yo-yo" pattern small table runner. Use pattern below. If you know a quilter, have them come in to show the participants how to make the yo-yo pattern table runner.

History:
The origin of yo-yo's has been credited to be China, but in the 500 B.C. the yo-yo was mentioned in Greek history. Regardless of who invented the first yo-yo, this toy became a big hit. Yo-yos are made from a variety of materials, such as wood, metal, or painted terra cotta, fashioned in a circle held together by a small ½-inch dowel, and a 30-inch string tied onto the dowel and wrapped until your fingers reached the discs. The top of the string had a loop that fit your middle finger, and then the fun can begin.

In the Philippines, they hunted with a type of yo-yo, as a weapon. A person climbed up a tree with a larger rock, the size of their fist, with a 20-foot twine wrapped around the rock. When an animal came by, that "yoyo" rock dropped on the animal while, holding onto the other end of the rope. Voila' Dinner!

The use of yoyos spread in China, Greece, and the Philippines, and later it went to India and the countries in Europe in 1765. India also made this fun toy for children and decorated the sides with a girl in a red dress playing with the yo-yo toy. Within 25 years, the yo-yo spread to Scotland, France, and England, but yoyos were mostly in the wealthy homes in these countries.

France started putting political advertising on the yoyo's, to advertise their favorite candidate. During King Louis XVII reign, the

French Revolution, and Reign of Terror, yo-yos were advertising tools. They came with a 4-year-old King Louis XVII picture on the sides. During this turbulent time, families fled France for Paris, Germany and other boarders carrying the small toy yo-yos with them. These yo-yos were made of glass and ivory during this time. These small toys caught on in these new countries as families fled France. In 1815, at the Battle of Waterloo, soldiers would play with yo-yos on their down time. Some even reported Napoleon playing with the toy yo-yo.

As the yo-yo continued to show up in the homes of the rich and famous, like Prince of Wales, the yo-yo grew in popularity. In 1866, the yo-yo arrived in the United States, and caught the eye of two Ohio investors who worked on a patent, which brought America the yo-yo. Charles Hettrick and Pedro Edralin Flores adjusted the patent, from the old yo-yo design, to include a loop instead of a knot on the axle, allowing the operator to perform the "sleep" trick along with many other tricks.

The fun part of the yo-yo is the variety of tricks that the operator can learn to perfect. Some of these tricks learned by children and adults alike are, walk the dog, the elevator, Eiffel Tower, rock the baby, round the world, forward toss, looping, UFO, and barrel roll, to name a few. Hours of entertainment spent learning these moves with the yo-yo providing entertainment for the operator as well as the spectators.

Donald F. Duncan Sr. used his first Flores brand yo-yo when he was in San Francisco, California. He saw Pedro doing a variety of tricks and drew mesmerizing crowds. While observing this interest in yo-yo's, businessman Duncan saw this as an opportunity build a yo-yo business. Duncan offered to purchase Pedro's yo-yo company and he sold it to him. In 1928, Donald Duncan built the popular Duncan Yo-Yo Company. Duncan employed professional yo-yo trick enthusiast to travel the United States demonstrating the yo-yo tricks. The Duncan Yo-yo Company took off and in 1932; he filed for a trademark for his yo-yo company. Yo-yo has had other names through the years, for instance: comeback, return, return top, whirl-a-gig, and twirler, but none of these names caught on like yo-yo.

The Duncan Yo-yo company moved to Luck, Wisconsin and became the "Yo-yo Capital of the World," producing 3,600 yo-yos per hour. The yearly production of yo-yos made from 1,000,000 feet of board, until 1962 when plastic yo-yos replaced wooden yo-yos. The Duncan Company still makes yo-yos for young and old to enjoy as they spend hours trying to perfect the yo-yo tricks. With the development of electronic toys, in 1965 the attraction of the yo-yo toy diminished causing the Duncan Yo-yo Company to go bankrupt.

In the 1970's, toy manufacturers reintroduced the yo-yo with a difference construction allowing the yo-yo to spin for better tricks and better movement for the "walking the dog" trick. With this new design, a renewed interest in the yo-yo was found which sparked new interest in the yo-yo. Educational videos now allowed the yo-yo operators to have private lessons anytime, day or night to perfect their tricks, making them able to draw a crowd to show off what they learned.

Activity:
- Get a bunch of yo-yos and have the participants try to work them. If you have anyone to show you how to be, fancy and do tricks.

Instructions: Yo-yo Quilt pattern, Small Table runner instructions.
(Use a volunteer quilt maker to help with this project)

1. The first step is to make your mind how large would you like your yo-yos to be and make a circular cutout template double that size plus about 1/2". A plastic or cardboard template works well enough.

2. Position the circle template on the right side of your fabric, if you are right-handed otherwise place it on the left and trace around it lightly with a pencil or chalk marker. Leave about 1/2" among circles.

3. Cut out circles about 1/4" past the line.

4. Thread a hand-sewing needle with *quilting thread*. If you use regular thread, sew with two strands. Knot the end of the thread and bring it up from the reverse side while folding under the circle on the line.

5. Continue sewing around the circle, folding under the seam allowance as you go.

6. When you reach the starting point, tug on the thread to gather the circle into a rosette. Leave a hole in the middle of the yo-yo.

7. Distribute the gathers and secure the thread with a few back stitches, then make a knot for extra security.

8. Trim excess thread, re-knot and make another yo-yo.

9. Arrange the yo-yos into rows and make them according t the selected design.

10. Next, sew two yo-yos. You can start from the center or from any side, as you would like to do. Repeat, adding more yo-yos to finish the row. Attach rows together in the same way.

11. Yo-yos can be sewn to a bigger piece of fabric, then layer with batting and bind around the edges.

FEBRUARY

Olympics

Food:
- Greek food, grape leaves rolled with rice or meat, Greek Salad, Gyro, Baklava, wedding cookies
- Decorate with a copy of the Olympic flag and display the metals that they will win.

Decorate:
- Make a Olympic Flag. White background with 5 rings: Red, Yellow, Blue, Green, and Black.
- Display metals: Gold, Silver and Bronze.

Crafts:
- Make ivy headpieces. For headpieces, use green construction paper or real ivy. Fashion them in a circular wreath, to fit on their heads. Ivy can be tied together periodically with small ribbon. Paper wreaths can be stapled together or glued. Fasten leaves on the the circular strip of green construction paper, or scrunched green tissue paper.
- Make Gold, Silver and Bronze Awards. Cut circles from the different colors of paper, and glue or staple them to red, white & blue ribbon, to put around participants necks as a metal.

History:
The origin of the first Olympics began 3,000 years ago in Olympia, Greece. The first games were from 776 BC through 393 AD, but then stopped until 1503 AD when they returned to Athens, Greece. One might wonder where the Olympic games got its name. The name derived from the location of where the first games were held, - Olympic, Athens. Organizers of the games thought this would be a good choice for the name for these games, since this is where the games originated. The games are rooted in the legend of Heracles, son of Zeus, and the mortal woman Alcmene. The games continued and by the end of the sixty century, the Olympics were the famous sporting competition festival for the Greek community. The schedule for the games were every four years to honor Zeus, and took place from August to September.

Originally Olympic Games were very different from today's Olympics. Baron de Coubertin from Paris brought the games back on January 1, 1863. Not having the games for 1,500 years, the games attracted 60,000 people to watch the various competitions.

The 280 participants from 13 nations, paraded on the field. Only men were allowed to compete or watch the Olympic games in the beginning. The main reason might be that they competed naked. Not even married women were let into the stands to observe these events. It was not until later, that men and women were allowed to watch the games, and uniforms for each country were required. Some of the summer games included: track and field events, gymnastics, swimming, wrestling, cycling, tennis, shooting, fencing, and weightlifting.

The ancient Olympics Games were held throughout Greece, but the modern Olympics are all around the world. The Summer Olympics are held every four years in the summer months, and the winter Olympics are held two years later, also on an every four years cycle. Both men and women compete in current Olympic Games. The Olympians team members proudly wear uniforms representing their countries, and woman and men still compete separately. Each team displays their county's uniform and flag proudly. The Gold, Silver and Bronze winners get their flag flown, while the Gold medalist has their National anthem played while they stand on the winners three-leveled platform. Olympians are proud to see their nation's flag flown and to hear their nation's Anthem played when they take the Gold medal. The only time the Olympic Games were canceled was during the World Wars.

In 1924, the Winter Olympics made its debut in Chamonix, France. The winter sports included figure skating, ice hockey, bobsledding, and the biathlon, to name a few. Later the winter sports included ski downhill racing, ski jumps and flips, cross country skiing, curling, figure skating, ice hockey and the luge.

You cannot see the Olympic Games without the Olympic torch and the five-ring flag. The tradition of the torch has a surprising origin. One would think that it originated in Greece, but the origin is from Nazi Germany. The flame brought to life by a parabolic mirror, kindling and the rays from the midday sun. This brought fire to the torch, which is use today, for the torch relay, in each opening of the Olympic Games. All who get to carry the torch feel honored to have been chosen.

The other famous symbol for the Olympics is the five interlocking rings flag. Each of the five rings represented five continents - North and

South America, Asia, Africa, Europe, and Australia. The Olympic rings features five colors - blue, black, red, yellow, and green on a white background. The different colors chosen for the rings to represent colors from each countries flag of the competing participants in the 1914 Olympic Games. This was the twentieth anniversary of the Olympic Games when this new tradition began featuring the Olympic Games flag.

Now try your luck at the "Olympic Games" for our participants to see who takes the Gold.

Activities:

- Set up various games that each participant must complete. 'Keep score for each participant, the one with the most points get the Gold medal, and next highest gets the Silver metal and the third highest gets the Bronze metal. Order medals or look at Dollar Stores for metals. You may have gold chocolate coins for all participants
  - Corn hole (ball toss), Have different points for the different holes.
  - Water guns and a lited candle. Time how long it takes for them to squirt it out.
  - Stacking cups. See who can get the highest stack in the shortest time.
  - Ladder Golf.
  - Blow the biggest soap bubble.
  - Paddle ball. Count how many times they can hit the ball and keep it going.
  - Balance a spoon on the end of their nose the longest.
  - Flip a tiddlywink into a cup. Count totals that get into the cups.
  - Bounce ping-pong balls into Solo cups. See the total number of balls that get in the cups.
  - Dress in togas
  - Olympic game completion puzzle. (See Attached)

Discovering George Washington Carver

Food:
- Peanuts, Peanut butter and crackers, Peanut butter and Jelly sandwiches. Coffee, tea, milk.

Crafts:
- Get peanuts in shells, white, red, blue, and green tempera paint, black sharpie marker, different colors of yarn for the scarfs, and small flat pieces of wood (2x5). Take the 4 - 5 peanuts and keep them in the shell, paint them white. On the top of the peanut, choose a color to paint them a skull hat. Use the sharpie to make the face. Paint the piece of wood white for snow. When the peanut people are dry, choose a color of yarn to use as a scarf. Then glue down your peanut snowman family on the piece of white painted wood for a fun winter decoration.

History:

Born into slavery on July 12, 1864, George Washington Carver went on to be a great inventor, scientist, and teacher. Carver was one of many children born to Mary and Giles Carver, but did not grow up with his other siblings, because he, his sister, and mom, were kidnapped one week after his birth when the farm where they lived and work was raided. The raiders took the three of them to Arkansas and sold them, and later sold them again to slave owners in Kentucky. His dad's owners, Moses, and Susan Carver had detectives looking for them and did not rest until they were found in Kentucky, and George brought them back to the farm in Missouri.

After the Civil War was over in 1865, George discovered that his slave owners, Moses, and Susan Carver were good people. The Carvers took good care of him and his brother James. Not only did they provide food, clothes, and housing, they educated them at home and taught them to read and write. This was special because no local schools that would allow black children to attend. After receiving this wonderful educational foundation, George left the home to study at a school that was ten miles away. His education allowed him to attend several schools, receiving his diploma from Minneapolis High School in Minneapolis, Kansas. He aspired to attend higher education after graduation and gained acceptance to Highland College in Highland, Kansas. When the college discovered George's race, they denied admittance.

George did not give up on his educational dreams; instead, he conducted biological experiments and compiled geological collections. George not only enjoyed the different scientific arenas, but he was also interested in the Arts, more specifically painting and drawing botanical sketches. George never gave up and in 1890, he was accepted and attended Simpson College in Iowa, studying Agriculture and Botanical Studies. His studies led him to a career as a brilliant botanist.

After graduating from Iowa State in 1896, George embarked on a teaching career at Tuskegee Institute running the School of Agriculture. This prestigious position, with a lucrative salary, developing the research and training of crop rotation, and the growth of the cash crop cotton. His research also helped control the boll weevils from destroying the cotton crops. George's research findings led to jobs for many former slaves, allowing their farms to become successful and secure for their families livelihoods. Black families began to flourish, and their children were learning how to be successful farmers too.

Along with farming, George provided mobile schools to come to the farms, providing children with education at their doorsteps. These schools got the nickname of "Jesup wagons." President Theodore Roosevelt, as well as the members of the British Royal Society of Arts recognized George's successful career, which is rare for Americans to receive. Indian leader, Mahatma Gandhi, trained and advised on successful planting of crops for a successful harvest, as well as sharing nutritional benefits of difference crops.

George developed many nutritional crops, which include sweet potatoes, soybeans, pecans, and the most famous plant was his peanut crops. As the popularity of these crops grew, George discovered that having a variety of crops, instead of just one, helped to return nutrients into the soil. As plants rotated their growing location each season, it prevented the lands from being stripped of its nutrients, providing a better crop   year after year. The years of just having cotton crops proved to deplete the soil, making a less substantial production of crops. George's research and inventions proved to assist sharecroppers in the South and former slaves, to provide productive farms for their families livelihood.

Many thought that George invented peanut butter since he developed the peanut crop, but it was not George. He did invent a form of peanut butter, but in 1890, a St. Louis physician invented the smooth, spreadable peanut butter that was packed in lunches all over the globe. In 1920, George delivered a speech to Congress, talking about the nutritional benefits of peanuts for health. After this speech, Carver was nicknamed, the "Peanut Man." George saw his development of the peanut and the invention of spreadable peanut butter as a possibility for racial harmony in United States, helping the peanut farmers and the health of the community. George joined with Booker T. Washington as activists for African American and White American relations.

George died on January 5, 1943, after falling down a flight of stairs at his home. He was 78 years old. His family buried him next to his friend, Booker T. Washington, on the grounds of Tuskegee Institute, where he was a professor and inventor. His epitaph said, "He could have added fortune to fame, but caring for neither, he found happiness and honor in being helpful to the world." So next time you eat a peanut or a peanut butter and jelly sandwich, remember George Washington Carver.

Activities:

- Use the letters **G E O R G E   W A S H I N G T O N   C A R V E R** and think of a poem using the first letter of his name to write it. E.g., G =Great E =Energetic etc. Or if you want to use a shorter word you could use **P E A N U T**

GEORGE WASHINGTON CARVER
POEM

G
E
O
R
G
E

W
A
S
H
I
N
G
T
O
N

C
A
R
V
E
R

P
E
A
N
U
T

History of Soup

Food:

- Different types of soups and toppers like shredded cheese and sour cream, and crackers.

Crafts:

- Pencil holder. Use small soup cans and decorate the outside with scrap booking paper. On the top and bottom edges, use ribbon to trim the top and bottom. Use a round piece of felt for the bottom so it will not scratch the table.

- Plant spices and herbs in soup cans. Get small soup scans; fill with dirt and plant spices or herbs like basil, mint, rosemary, parsley, and/or cilantro. Participants can use them to cook or accent foods. Herbs have great nutritional benefits and helps the brain and body too. These cans can be left with the soup labels for fun or covered with paper and labeled what the spice/herb is on the containers.

History:

Can you think back to when you were a child, and the snow began to fall? Your mom would put on a pot of potato soup to warm your body up after you played in the snow. The smell of the soup would fill the house with wonderful aromas. She would begin with sauteing onions and celery in butter and add some flour to make a paste for the white sauce. She would add milk, cubed potatoes and let it simmer for an hour or two. Then she would serve it to you with shredded cheese and bacon bits, for a wonderfully warm and filling taste treat. Those memories stay with until today.

When soup began, it was nothing like our soups of today. Originally, soups were a rather watery gruel broth. Cooked from ground, roasted cereal poured over bread is how soup originated. The bread would be used to "sop" or "sup" up the broth, and that is what it was originally called, and which later became "soup." Broth, pottage, or gruel are still used in some cultures, and are made with legumes, chestnuts, or root vegetables. This early soup resembled the porridge of the three bears in the Goldie Locks story.

People of all income levels and countries have made soup for centuries. Typically, soup began with a trip to the cabinet to see what ingredients were available. During difficult times, ingredients were hard to come by and soup was an economical way to use leftover meat or vegetables without waste.

The favorite soup for most cultures is the chicken soup that your mom made you when you were sick. Hot soup opens up sinuses, thins out mucus, soothes sore throats, and helps with hydration. Warm chicken soup is a sure ticket to feel better, breath more easily, and help you along the road to recovery.

Favorite soups are as varied as the cultures and regions of the world. In Spain, gazpacho soup is popular and nutritious. The ingredients include; cucumber, bell pepper, red onion, jalapeno, garlic, clove, olive oil, lime juice, balsamic vinegar, Worcestershire sauce, cumin, salt and pepper that are blended together and served cold. It is a favorite soup served in the heat of the summer.

Russia's traditional soup is borscht. If you do not like beets, this would not be the soup for you. You peel three mediums to large size beets and grate into a pot. Add olive oil, low sodium chicken broth and water, Yukon potatoes peeled and cubed, and two carrots sliced thin, cabbage, dill, red wine vinegar, sour cream, and beef shank bone. This soup is a little more time consuming but is worth the effort for another good tasting soup.

Italian cooks are famous for their minestrone soup. This delicious soup made with onion, garlic, celery, carrots, green beans, oregano, basil, ground pepper, diced tomatoes, crushed tomatoes, chicken broth, elbow pasta, Parmesan cheese and topped with fresh basil. Many restaurants have this well-loved soup on their menus.

In eighteenth century, Paris served their famous Onion soup in the first restaurant. Most of their soups were clear broths or consummés. Etiquette experts insisted that soups eaten with a spoon is proper etiquette, and never slurped or not drunk from the bowl. Since this was difficult to do without spilling, soups began having other ingredients like noodles, rice, and vegetables. Nowadays, soups come in convenient packaging for people to take it to work for a quick lunch. Most instant soups you just add water and heat in a microwave and eat. What is your favorite soup?

Activities:

- Make different types of soup or have everyone bring in a different type of soup. You may want to do this activity first to enjoy during your session.
- Read the story. *"Stone Soup."*

MARCH

Mr. Rogers and His Neighborhood

Food:

- Trail mix ("cat food"), Cupcakes with kitty cat ears, crowns, and tiger ears.

Crafts:

- Mr. Rogers had several puppets. King Friday XIII, Daniel Striped Tiger, X the Owl, Henrietta Pussycat, to name a few. Choose one to make as a sock puppet.

- You could just make crown for King Friday XIII, or cat ears on a headband, or Striped Tiger on a headband.

- Make a candy train. Begin with a 5-stick package of gum, glue a package of Lifesavers on top of the gum package, use peppermint for the 4 wheels, a candy kiss for the front top of the life saver package, and 2 stacked Rollo's on top of the back of the life saver for where the conductor drives the train. Mr. Roger has the train station in his neighborhood, and this will represent that aspect of the program.

Ingredients:

- 1 roll of Lifesavers Candy

- 1 small package of gum

- 1 chocolate Rollo Candy

- 1 Hershey's Kiss

- 1 mini Hershey's chocolate bar

- 1 Starburst candy

- 4 Round peppermint candies

- Fancy string or Ribbon for the ornament hanger

- Low temp. hot glue gun

How to make it

- To make a train as an ornament, tie a ribbon into a loop around the Lifesavers.

- Glue the roll of Lifesavers candy to the package of gum with the ribbon loop in-between.

- Glue the peppermint candies on each side to make the wheels of the Candy Train.

- Glue the Hershey's Kiss on the end of the Lifesavers to make the train smokestack. (I do mine with the flat side up but I have seen them the other way)

- On the other end of the train glue a Rollo candy to make the engineer's room - glue a small candy on top for the roof (use a Starburst candy or mini chocolate bar)

- Take your mini Hershey's bar and run a bead of glue the entire length and place on back end of the Candy Train.

- *These are adorable additions to holiday gift baskets and also good stocking stuffers.

History:

A famous Presbyterian Minister, children's television storyteller, puppeteer, writer, and producer of Mr. Roger's Neighborhood was a wonderful man, Fred McFeely Rogers. He was born Latrobe, Pennsylvania, near Pittsburgh, March 20, 1928 and died on February 27, 2003. This kind, soft-spoken, gentle host of the preschool children's, program taught children life lessons on how to treat others by using his characters from his make believe "neighborhood." His long running preschool series ran from 1968 to 2001.

Fred Rogers had a bachelor's degree in music from Rollins College in 1951 and began his television career that year with NBC in New York. He decided to return to Pittsburgh in 1953 and changed networks to NET, which later became what we know as PBS. Fred then decided to go to Pittsburgh Theological Seminary, studying to be a Presbyterian minister, graduating in 1963. Following graduation, he studied at the University of Pittsburgh for a Graduate degree in Child Development.

Upon graduation, Fred worked with child psychologist Margaret McFarland to develop several children's productions including, The Children's Corner," in 1955, followed by "Mister Rogers" in 1968, and everyone's favorite "Mister Rogers' Neighborhood," which ran for 33 years. During this show, Fred dealt with difficult issues facing kids, like divorce, bulling, sibling rivalry and death. He also introduced sensitive issues like prejudice, inclusion and belonging.

Although Fred received 40 honorary degrees and several awards, the Lifetime Achievement Emmy in 1987, Television Hall of Fame in 1999, and the Presidential Medal of Freedom in 2002, Fred remained humble, always looking out for the best interest of others. He was sensitive and perceptive about what others might be going through. This may have been do to his experience being bullied as an child due to his weight.

Unfortunately, his life was not always easy, and neither was the end of his story. He suffered and died at the age of 74, from stomach cancer. This beloved man, gave preschoolers and the world some place to go where they could feel loved, accepted, wanted, and included, - everything everyone really wants in life.

Activities:

- Watch an episode of Mister Rogers Neighborhood.
- Watch the Documentary of Mr. Rogers life.
- Word search of Mister Rogers Neighborhood characters.

MR. ROGERS NEIGHBORHOOD PUZZLE

```
B E B T B S T S Y T W H H L Y
A U W C V M J R V A E G Z N D
N T Z R Y B E E O G D R W S E
E J T W E V L G X L C I E X E
C S A E I E O O U V L A R Q P
O U V L I L Q R M M F E B F S
R V E N C R Y R N C B F Y J H
T D A O N R N M O F O K K N S
S D F L S J M E Z E G N I T B
T I G E R H L X H E I O R N Q
D L I H C R I A F L H I L M G
A A B S P T R V R Y P M V N I
V H W F N L D T E E L T S A C
X N I I T J B R D K N K P I A
P U S S Y C A T H W P Y Q W X
```

CASTLE	DANIEL	DELIVERY
FAIRCHILD	FRIDAY	HENRIETTA
KING	MCFEELY	MRROGERS
PUSSYCAT	SPEEDY	STRIPED
TIGER	TROLLEY	

National Butterfly Day – March 14

Food:

- Make butterfly shaped cookies, icing and decorate. Cut cheese wedges in triangles and put pretzels in the center as the body. Cut apples in slices and use carrots for the body. Serve soda, coffee, tea, or lemonade.

Craft:

- Several coffee filters, and pipe cleaners (for each participant), markers to share, magnets with sticky back. Color the coffee filters as desired, then spritz with water to allow the colors to run together. Let them dry. When dry, fold in half and scrunch the top and bottom together at the fold. Then twist the pipe cleaner at about two-inch length, leaving two ends for the antennas. You have a butterfly. You can put a magnet on the back to stick on the refrigerator. Each participant can make several.

- Wax paper, tissue paper cut in small pieces, pipe cleaner, magnets with sticky back. Have participant glue tissue paper on the wax paper in any design. When dry, cut out the butterfly shape using the pattern below. You can make different sizes if you prefer. Use the pipe cleaner to make a body and antenna. (See directions above). Stick magnet on back of butterfly.

History:

As we think about Spring, our thoughts move to the gardens with lovely flowers and butterflies. Butterflies floating around our gardens are a beautiful addition to see. These insects go through quite the changes to transform into this lovely butterfly, as we know them.

This lovely insect has four phases that they must go through to reach its beautiful flying insect. It begins as an egg. Their mothers lay these eggs on milkweed plant leaves. The adult butterfly stick their eggs to leaves with a special glue they produce. The eggs take 3 days to hatch. When they emerge from their egg stage, they are caterpillars. The caterpillars eat off the milkweed plant for 10-12 days before encasing themselves in chrysalides' pods. The chrysalis's pods hold the transforming butterflies for 7-10 days. Before they emerge, they attach themselves to a suitable twig or sturdy leaf for a few hours to allow their body to fill with blood and dry off. After this process is complete, they can finally fly, making their debut as beautiful butterflies we enjoy.

Depending on the specie of butterfly, they can live from one week to one year.

Mourning Cloaks, some tropical Heliconians, and monarch butterflies are some of the longer living butterflies species. Butterflies have four wings, adorned with vibrant colors. Their heads have two antennas and a proboscis coming from their mouth to suck up liquid food from flowers and plants. The rest of their body has four legs, 2 attached to their thorax, and 2 attached to the abdomen. On the bottom of their feet, they have taste receptors to identify nectar on the flowers.

What attracts us to butterflies is their unique bright colored wings. These colors are made of tiny scales. Scientist have discovered that there are 15,000 to 20,000 species of butterflies. A unique butterfly is the Birdwing. This specie has angular wings and fly like birds. (find a photo of a Birdwing to show)

The most familiar butterfly is the Monarch, with its black and bright orange wings. Each year Monarchs travel great distances, sometimes over 2,485 miles, just to lay their eggs. Interestingly, the females lay their eggs and the new hatched butterflies will travel back to their parent's original location. Monarch butterflies are the only known specie that migrates.

We think of bees when we think of animals that help to pollinate our plants. But the butterfly along with the bees, and bats, help with this important process. Flowers, fruits, and vegetables would not be as plentiful without these pollinator animals. Many individuals will choose specific plants to plant in their gardens, to attract butterflies for their enjoyment. In fact, we need them, but they need us for survival too. Planting the right flowers helps the butterflies get the nutrients they need to survive. Depending on what food is available, determines on how long they can survive.

Learning about butterflies, may make you want to visit a butterfly farm, or plant bushes that will attract and feed these beautiful floating wonders in your yard.

Activities:

- Make butterfly shaped cookies and decorate them with beautiful colored icings. Use a toothpick to swirl the icing to make beautiful designs.

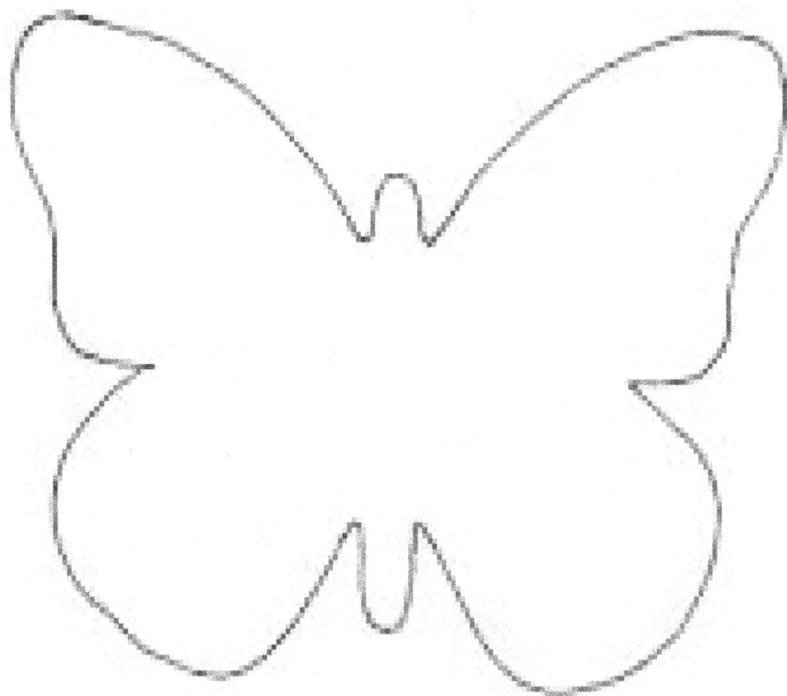

Discovering your Senses

Food:
- Different types of cookies. This will arouse all the senses if you make the cookies together.
- Different types of pie.
- Different types of teas.

Decorations:
- Different pretty photos of landscapes, families, babies, or flowers. You can get them out of magazines as a group, or have them glued on 5x7 pieces of paper.

Crafts:
- You will need different colors of tissue paper, green pipe cleaners, and scissors. To make tissue paper flowers. Take four pieces of tissue paper and cut it in half down the length of the paper. It can be the same color or different colors. Fold the shorter end back and forth in 1-inch folds until the end. You then have a fan. Take pipe cleaner and twist it tight in the center of the folds. Allow the fan to open up and separate each tissue paper making it look like a flower pedal.

History:

The world as we know it revolves around our five senses, and this is how we get our information from the world around us. At first, we open our eyes and see the beautiful nature all around. Light is the key to sight. The rays of light reflect off an object and goes through the cornea in the front of our eye. The cornea has a transparent cover of protection. The retina converts the light into the image that sends a message to our brains. An interesting fact is that the image is upside down on the retina, but our brains turn the image around. The light comes from millions of light sensor cells called rods and cones. The rods are for monochrome vision in poor lighting, and the cones provide us with color. When all our senses are working, the eyes provide 75% of our information of our world around us.

Our ears provide 13% of what we learn from our world around us. Sound waves enter our ears and travel through a passageway called the ear canal. The canal leads to the eardrum, which is a tightly stretched flap of skin that works like a musical drum sending vibrations to the middle ear. The middle ear has three small bones, the malleus, incus, and stapes, which vibrate in a way to transfer the sound waves to your cochlea, and onto the brain to hear the world around us. We can hear birds chirping, babies laughing and our favorite music.

The third sense is our sense of smell. Our nose can help us smell a wonderful flower like roses, a favorite food like bacon or fresh bread baking, or to warn us about something dangerous like a gas leak. As air passes through your nose, it passes over olfactory cells, to olfactory bulbs, which sends what we smell to the brain. The nose helps us know 80% of the flavors we taste and enjoy. When we have a cold the flavors, we smell are diminished so we cannot taste the food we are trying to enjoy.

Without smell, our taste is not as strong. Our tongues have many taste buds that identifies sweet, sour, bitter, salty and umami, which is meaty and savory items. When we take a bite of our food, the taste buds are stimulated and send messages to our brain to identify the flavors. Scientists think our craving sweet or salty foods is a biological preference, determined by your DNA. Therefore, some of us prefer sweet foods while others prefer salty ones. No matter what our preferences are, the taste sense is a wonderful part of our five senses.

The last sense is touch. Our skin contains millions of nerve endings and receptors along our skin called the somatosensory system. These receptors and nerve endings help us to feel cold, hot, smooth, rough, pressure, tickle, itchy, pain, vibrations and more. When we feel a sensation on our skin of pain, the bottom dermis layer of our skin is responsible to send the message to our brain. If we feel an ant crawling on our arm, the epidermis, or outer layer feels the gentle touch, also sending a message to our brain to knock the bug off, This 46 miles of nerves communicates both enjoyable and painful events so that we can respond appropriately.

Our bodies are very interesting. If we lose one of our senses, our brain turns to the remaining senses and focus on strengthening other senses to compensate for that loss. For example, if you lose your sight, your ears become more sensitive to hear the world around you. We are so fortunate to have such an amazing body of senses to experience our world.

Activities:

- Get a variety of smells: Lemon, peppermint, chocolate, honeysuckle, lavender, rose, garlic, onion. Have the participants guessed the smells.
- Put different objects in a bag or box and have the participants try to guess what they are touching without looking. Objects could include sandpaper, bubble wrap, cotton ball, kitchen whisk, spatula, potato peeler, Emory board, toothbrush, comb, tweezers, nail clippers, etc.
- Have foods to taste. For example, orange, chocolate, popcorn, pudding, gumdrop, peanut butter, cherry, lemon, and peppermint. Reminisce about the smells and tastes and what memories they inspire.
- You can play different instruments to see if they can identify them.

History of Quilting

Food:

- Different types of Teas, shortbread cookies, finger sandwiches, to simulate a ladies quilting tea.

Craft:

- Quilted place mat. Collect several different colors of cotton fabric. Cut six - 6-inch squares of the colors you choose, alternating the materials to make the design more interesting. You can cut the squares smaller if you want for a more involved pattern. (e.g., cutting 12 - 3x3 blocks, alternating colors, or patterns of fabric.) Then cut two - 2 inch by 16 1/2-inch strips, and then cut two 2 inches by 18 1/2-inch strips. The shorter strips sew vertically on the place mat and the longer strips sew onto the horizontal side of the place mat. The strips will frame the place mat. Begin to hand stitch the blocks to together in an alternating color patter. If you have a sewing machine, you can stitch them on the machine. Make sure the seams are all going in the same direction, leaving a clean look on the top side of the place mat. When all the sewing is completed, use a sturdy interfacing the same size of the finished front of the place mat to add stiffness to your mat. Then cut a piece of cotton fabric of your choice to the same size of the quilted side and the interfacing piece. When the bottom of the place mat is cut to match the size of the top, pin the right sides together and sew around the entire place mat, leaving an opening about 5 inches to pull the place mat right-side out. Take a pin to pull out the corners to make them 90% angles. Hand stitch the 5 inches closed. Iron the place mat down smooth, and then you are ready to use your place mat.

- If this above quilted place mat is too difficult, try finding fabric that looks like a quilt pattern. Then cut two pieces into 12 1/2 by 18 1/2 inches. Then cut a piece of stiff stabilizer the same size to put inside the place mats. Next, sew the right sides together, with the stabilizer between the top and bottom of mat. Make sure to leave 5-inch opening to turn the fabric right side out. Take a needle and pull out the corners until they make the corners square. Then iron the place mat flat and sew up the unsewn edge. You can use ribbon or rickrack to decorate around the place mat for fun.

History:

In many homes starting from 3400 BC until today, you will find a beautiful, handmade quilt. These beautifully designed layers of fabrics, with batting padding between, creates a warm blanket. Not only were quilts used for blankets, but they were also used for protection, insulation from the cold as well as wall decorations. Some of the wall decoration designs might include special moments like weddings or birth of a child, they may memorialize a loved one who has died or may depict one's political view. No doubt, women, and some men, gathered favorite patterns of cotton fabrics, and put them together to create beautiful pieces of art.

In the early 1800's, food such as flour, and sugar, came in decorative cotton fabric bags. The fabric which housed these food items, were the main fabrics utilized for clothing as well as quilting. Scraps of fabric left from making a garment were assembled in beautiful patterns for quilts. These scraps become beautiful works of art, whether it is a wall hanging, a table runner, or keeping you warm decorating the top of your bed, quilts were as popular then as they are today.

Many groups of women would come together to work on a quilt, these groups are called; "Quilting Bees." In the 19th century, so many women would pass the time on the open plains by making quilts and other items that they could use in their homes. Quilting Bees were quite the social event for women traveling by wagons on the prairies. Some women would travel many miles to other camps, to work on a quilt. Quilting Bees also became mentoring times for older women to teach the younger women not only quilting, but cooking and child rearing skills. The Quilting Bee groups would make quilts for newlywed couples or for others in need. Today, groups of women in churches or other social groups would come together for a joint project too. Some of these projects might be to make quilts for the beds of the Rescue Mission individual, to give to orphans, healing quilts for ill friends and family members, or to give to someone sick in a nursing home. No matter if it was 3400 BC or today, Quilting Bees provides great opportunities to socialize with a purpose, interest, and goal in mind, while developing great friendships and having fun.

In the fifteenth century, Sweden's quilts used more appliques and heavier, broad stitches. The appliques usually had a theme like flowers, birds, or places of interest. Quilts were usually made for the wealthy in Sweden, and were not made from scrap fabrics, rather expensive fabrics like silk wool, or felt were used. Quilts used not only in homes of noblemen, but also in local churches as religious decorations on the walls and alters.

There are many patterns designs for quilts that many quilters use. Some designs are: Log Cabin, Flying Geese, Star, Patchwork, Nine Patch, Bear Paw, and Traditional Celtic Square. Quilters are always making up new designs for special quilts. Whether you love and enjoy quilting, or have no interest in making them, everyone can agree that that quilts are beautiful and functional works of art.

Activities:
- Word Search with quilting focus.
- Get photos of different quilt pattern to see if the group can name them

HISTORY OF QUILTING

```
L J G R R G R M N J N N P S M
E C P A A K R Q T O Y A F I S
J I G T L T U A G U T Z T M K
T R B S G P S A N C I R Y P U
R C F H X G X E H N A L T L F
X L Y G E E J W N D Y I E I E
R E Q I H R O M E O G R U C X
Z F Q H R R M D X W L X V I E
H I L A K S D N I W S W F T N
X F P A E U G A E L Y V I Y P
G T N K H G T T A U I S L U N
R E A Z G R A S C J Q A U R O
V E Q Z E P E W Z X K G C C K
S Q U A R E R N S X G Z H S M
O Y S T X K A Z I H G D L I I
```

CIRCLE	GRANNY	HALF
HEXAGON	HIGHSTAR	IVY LEAGUE
LONESTAR	PATCHWORK	SIMPLICITY

APRIL

National Poetry Day

Food:

Appetizer foods like Peach Salsa and Chips, Cheese and crackers, veggie tray and dip.

Crafts:

- Illustrate your poem. Type or write the poem on paper to add to your drawing.

- Write a Hakiu poem and illustrate it. You can use free style poetry, Haiku Poem (3 lines of 5-7-5 syllables).

Example:

> **The wind caught my hat**
> **Away it blew from my head**
> **Isn't summer fun**

- Rhyming poems like Dr. Seuss, or just written thoughts can also be fun.

History:

Poetry as an art form predates written text. Early recited poetry was a way to keep oral history, genealogy, and laws to pass on, sometimes presented as a song. As you hear some hymns, you see they have poetic lyrics. Dr. Seuss had the art form of rhythmic rhyming that would last his entire storybook. Poems help people remember thoughts, prayers, and ideas in their heart. Valentine's Day people write their thoughts for their loved ones usually in the form of a poem. One that comes to mind that most people remember is "Roses are Red, Violets are Blue, Sugar is Sweet, and so are you." Schoolteachers will use poetry to help students remember facts and history. Poems give people a way to remember Bible verses especially in the King James Version of the Bible.

African history shows poetry in the prehistoric times. In the 25th century BC, writings shows poetic verses in Pyramid texts. Traditionally, African dances and performances linked to poetry, which makes the message of traditions, political views, educational, traditions of life and spirituality as well as for entertainment.

The oldest surviving poem is the *Tale of the Shipwrecked Sailor*. Written around 2500 B.C.E. (you could read this poem here). Different shorter versions can be found online or order the child's book with photos.

Types of Poetry:

- Narrative Poems: A poem that tells a story, it is longer than lyric style poems, and has characters and a plot
- Ode: A formal, often ceremonious lyric that celebrates a person, place, thing, or idea
- Epic: A long narrative poem in which a heroic protagonist engages in an action of great mythic or historical significance.
- Prose poem: A prose is not broken into verse lines, but has poetic symbols, metaphors, and other figures of speech common to poetry.
- Lyric: Musical verse, expresses observations and feeling of a single speaker
- Sonnet: 14-line lyric poem
- Shakespearean: Has three quatrains and a couplet.
- Hakiu Poetry: A Japanese poem consisting of three short lines. The first and third lines have 5 syllables and the second line has 7 syllables. They do not have to rhyme.

Activities:

- Set up the room like a poetry reading. Have the participants read their poem and show their picture. Look up and read poems from your favorite poets or have the participants read them.

- Have the participants read their poems and show their illustrations. Or if they do not want to read them, you read them and show their illustrations.

- List some poets and make a word search with their names. Edgar Allen Poe, Shakespeare, Emily Dickerson, Ralph Waldo Emerson, William Yeats, Wordsworth, John Milton, Robert Frost, John Keats, E.E. Cummings, T.S. Eliot, Mark Twain (to name a few)

National Umbrella Day.
February 10

Food:

- Apples, bending straws, circle cheese. Slice the apple in half from top to bottom, then slice the half apple in half from side to side. Take out the seeds. Cut the plastic straws to make a umbrella handle and then turn the bendy part so it looks like an umbrella handle.

- Cut circle cheese and use plastic picks for umbrella handles. Fold the circle cut cheese in half, and in forth, and put the plastic picks between two layers of the cheese to make it look like a folded (down position) umbrella.

- Mocktails. Use small plastic clear party cups, orange juice, pineapple juice, grenadine syrup, cherries, chunky pineapples, slice of an orange and a little paper umbrellas. Recipe for mocktail: 4 ounces orange juice, 3 ounces pineapple juice, 1-ounce grenadine syrup, and ice. Put cherry and pineapples chunk in the bottom of a small clear party glass, and decorate the glass with a paper umbrella, orange slice for the rim of the glass for garnish.

Craft:

- Construction paper for each person, contrasting color for the umbrellas, umbrella pattern and poem. Alternatively, see **Activities** section to write your own poem. See bottom of page for umbrella pattern and poem.

History:

When it is "raining cats and dogs," you will be glad for the invention of the umbrella. The Chinese first invented this most useful accessory over 4,000 years ago. Egyptian and Greek artifacts show umbrella findings during that same period. Earlier umbrellas designs were to keep off the heat of the sun. Some earlier umbrellas did not collapse but were used for shading on chariots. In China, umbrellas were accessories and decoration for one's outfit. Some umbrellas used for sunshade where made from paper with elaborate designs.

You see an entire row of umbrellas lining the beach front hotels, to keep the heat of the day off the beach-goers. This wonderful invention assist fair skin beach-goers from getting painful sunburns. We also see little paper umbrellas decorating our tropical drinks, while vacationers sit by the pool, enjoying a cold drink.

Today we associate using an umbrella mostly when it is raining. Perhaps you can remember the iconic scene from the 1952 movie, "Singing in the Rain," when Gene Kelly danced in the rain, around the lamppost and in puddles. Whenever the weather predicts storms, we reach for an umbrella to go with us to work or run errands.

Umbrellas used for rain were developed by the Chinese culture. A layer of wax melted over the paper and topped with a coat of lacquer to repel rainwater was the first materials for rain umbrellas. The development of this process brought another use for the umbrella. Chinese use decorative umbrellas for celebrations, and the lovely decorated umbrellas dance in the parade at Chinese New Year's. New Orleans Mardi Gras parades and funerals have decorative umbrellas adorning the parade routes too.

Umbrellas show up in artwork, parades, and movies. Another popular movie with an umbrella was in 1964, when Mary Poppins floated into the scene to apply as a nanny position for Jane and Michael Banks. The wind carried all the others applying for the job away as the umbrella landed Mary Poppins as the only candidate for the job at the Bank's front door. Mary Poppins umbrella had a talking bird handle that provided witty banter with Mary Poppins throughout the movie.

The word Umbrella is a Latin word that means "shade," or "shadow." In the late nineteenth century, the slang word "bumbershoot," used in America as a whimsical word for umbrellas. Britain, New Zealand, Australia, and South Africa used a slang word "brolly," for umbrella. French women call an umbrella that shields them from the sun, a "parasol."

James Smith and Sons opened the first umbrella shop in London, England in 1830. Umbrellas are used often in England due to their rainy climate, a great business opportunity for the Smith brothers. This store is still in operation at 53 New Oxford Street in London. In 1928, Hans Haupt invented a pocket size umbrella. Pocket size umbrellas were developed, patented, produced and sold in Ohio. This convenient size umbrella became very popular to hide in a backpack, briefcase, or large purse. Some ladies like to change their umbrellas to match or accent their outfits.

You may see photographers of supermodels using umbrellas as an accent piece in their photos for magazine. Their photographers use white umbrellas to help adjust their lighting in order to get just the right light to make their photos pop.

Activities:

- Write a Haiku poem. Begin constructing the three lines of the haiku poem. The first line must have **five syllables**; the second line must have seven and the third line five for 17 syllables in the entire poem. Add this poem to your umbrella craft.

Pattern: Use pipe cleaners or popsicle stick for handle of the umbrella

National Story Telling Day

Food:

- Old time candies. This could be part of the activity. Have the group tell the first time they had that candy.

- Popcorn like you would get when you are watching a movie.

Crafts:

- Get a mason jar for each person. Write words or phrases on small slips of paper and put them in the jar. You can do one jar for the group and have everyone contribute to the story or have everyone make up their individual story and share with the group. You can decorate the jar with "Story Telling Jar," sign. This jar could remain on the table for future activities.

- Write a story and make props for the story you wrote. (e.g., A crown, scepter, cap etc. if it is a castle story)

History:

All around the world you see families and friends sitting around the table, campfire or at parties hearing and sharing stories of days gone by. We all enjoy learning how our parents met, or adventures they experienced throughout their life. National Storytelling observance began in 1990's in Sweden, and soon caught on around the world. Oral history is a great way to keep stories alive and to pass history to the next generation. The Bible is a great example of oral history. At first the lessons and parables were not written down, at least not until 300 AD. Later this information was compiled in scrolls and then later in the Bible book.

Storytelling comes in many forms, read from a book, created from one's imagination, or from an actual life experience. This ancient practice is fun for the storyteller and the listening audience. Children love to hear a bedtime story, either read or made up, which bridges the gap between the hearer and storyteller. Spending time storytelling helps us grow closer to our family and to our friends.

Some storytellers are so engaging they have the audience hanging on every word of the story. Some storytellers keep their audience laughing or in suspense for the outcome. Storytelling is an art form that hopes to engage the imagination of the listener in a way that they can see the story in their imagination.

Storytelling is interaction between a storyteller and an audience of one or more. Storytellers hope to grab the attention of their audience immediately, before leading them down their story path. Some stories are hidden within the jokes, movements, or gestures until you get to the punch line. Contemporary storytelling may use puppets, drama, music, dance, pantomime, and a variety of props to convey the story they are telling the audience. Some groups use props and engage the audience to help create and improvisation story for fun entertainment.

Many cultures have different forms and venues for storytelling, but no matter what props or forms used for the storytelling process, everyone likes to hear and tell a good stories.

Activities:

- Write a store, individually or as a group. Suggested ideas for story plots: Conquering a Monsters, Rags to Riches, Dragon and Princess Quest, Tragedy, An Adventure and Return from the adventure, or Comedy. To plan the ending of the story you can consider: Happy ending, Unhappy ending, or Tragedy (like Romeo and Juliet)
- You can use "Madd Libs." These are stories that have you add, nouns, verbs, adverbs, and adjectives. Once you have filled in the needed items, the story is ready to read aloud to the group. You can also find these stories online.

National Peace Rose Day

Food:

- Citrus Rose Water Tea

  1 Earl Grey Tea Bag
  1 medium orange, thinly sliced
  3 tablespoons white sugar
  1 teaspoon rose water

- Prepare a strong cup of tea with the Earl Grey, letting the bag steep for 5 minutes. Place the orange slices, sugar, rose water, and tea into a ½-gallon pitcher, fill with cold water, and stir to dissolve the sugar. Rose water can be purchased at Walmart or Amazon.

- Make a pound cake in a rose shaped Bundt pan.

- Pepperoni Roses

  Crescent Dough Sheet
  Pizza Sauce
  Pepperoni
  Shredded Cheese

Roll out your sheet of dough. Use a pizza cutter to cut in in one-inch strips. Add pizza sauce to each strip, and line up pepperoni along the strips of dough letting one side hang off the dough. Sprinkle shredded cheese along each strip. Roll each dough up from one end of the strip to the other, making a flower. Place each flower into a muffin tin. Bake at 375 degrees for 13 minutes or until golden brown. Once done, let them cool a bit. Then serve and enjoy!

Decorations: Doves for the symbol for Peace, bouquets of roses, Rose sachet or rose scent oils or sprays.

Crafts:
- Copy a clipart outline of a rose on the internet. Then copy the rose outline on watercolor paper so it fits on an 8½ X 11-size paper. Using light yellow or cream-colored watercolor paint, color the main part of the rose with this color leaving the edges of the rose pedals white. After you finish the yellow/cream color, use a crimson, pink color for the edges of the pedals. After you finish, let the rose dry. When the photo is dry, use a mat and frame to display the art project.

History:

On April 29, each year is the celebration day for a beautiful light yellow/beige rose with crimson, pink on the tip of the pedal edges. This beautiful rose known as the Peace Rose. They chose the name because the Peace Rose development took place between 1935 and 1939 during World War II. The developer of the rose was a French horticulturist, Francis Meilland, who originally called the rose 3 – 35 – 40.

As WWII was ending, Francis Meilland did not want this beautiful rose to be lost, so he had the forethought to send cuttings to his horticulture friends in Germany, Italy, Turkey and the United States. His idea to send these clippings to other countries to his horticulture friends was the saving act for this beautiful rose. As you travel the world, you see the hardy, beloved Peace Rose displayed in many personal and community gardens throughout the world.

In the beginning, each country had different names for the lovely rose. In France, Francis Meilland named his rose "Gloria," meaning Joy, in honor of his mother. Germany called the rose "Gloria Dei," meaning to the Glory to God. The United States thought since World War II ended, the best name for this rose would be to call it the "Peace Rose," and that is the favorite name for this lovely rose.

These beautiful rose blooms are five inches across in diameter. The leaves are dark green with a glossy shine. The Peace Rose has become one of the bestselling roses purchased for gardens around the world because of this hardy nature. California Pacific Rose Society of Pasadena chose *The Peace Rose*, as a favorite flower for the Tournament of Roses Parade. I am sure that Francis Meilland was very proud of his development of this rose. On April 29, 1947, the Peace Rose received the National Gold Medal Certificate, and in

1965, this beautiful rose receives the Gold Rose of the Hague award. The Peace Rose accompanied a handwritten note to each of the delegates at the first United Nation meeting in San Francisco, in 1945. This gesture made a significant claim for notoriety for this rose, especially with the note read; "We hope the Peace Rose will Influence men's thoughts for everlasting world peace."

Thirty to forty million Peace rose bushes produced and purchased each year. This hardy, disease resistant, Peace Rose has been a popular plant for many Peace Gardens built around the world. These gardens and rose commemorate the 50 years of peace since German surrender in World War II. Therefore, if you are looking for a beautiful rose to add to your garden, you might want to consider the Peace Rose for your next garden addition.

Activities:
- Purchase some small Peace Rose plants and clay pots to decorate. Decorate clay pot, or use paper designs of red, white, and blue to accent the pots. These designs could represent our troops for their brave service and successful winning the war. The group as an act of appreciation could deliver these flowers to the VA Hospital.

- Patriotic Bingo. Play the following patriotic songs and have bingo sheets with the different songs listed In different squares. Whoever wins could get a small American Flag. Songs: The Star-Spangled Banner, God Bless America, You're a Grand Ol' Flag, Battle Hymn of the Republic, This is My Country, The Corps, Army Strong, National Spirit March, The Army Goes Rolling Along, Anchors Aweigh, Off We Go Into the Wild Blue Yonder, The Marines' Hymn, Sound Off Air Force Blue, The Stars and Stripes Forever, This Land is Your Land, God Bless the U.S.A., America – My Country Tis of Thee, America The Beautiful.

- Create Bingo pages from this web site:

  https://wordmint.com/pages/landing/bingo?headline=Bingo+Card+Creator&_puzzle_type=Bingo&bing_loc_physical_ms=87097&msclkid=e66a508918cf185758070f5369f26955&utm_source=bing&utm_medium=cpc&utm_campaign=bing.wordmint.bingo.phrase&utm_term=create%20your%20own%20bingo&utm_content=phrase.bingo_creator

The Use of Idioms

Food:
- Jelly Belly Jellybeans with the surprising flavors. You think you are eating one flavor and discover the taste is different than you expect.

Crafts:
- Order or purchase from hobby shop small drawstring bags at least 5X7. The bags can be larger but not too much smaller. The bag need not to be see through, rather plain cotton or burlap. You could enlist someone to make them, they would be simple to make. One one side of the bag, paint a Tic-Tac-Toe board, or you could glue down strips of felt to make the playing board. Gather or purchase smooth rocks, 12 per person to make half with X's and the other half with O's painted on them. When they are dry, tuck inside the bag. This can be a nice pass time while waiting at a restaurant to be seated. It is small and could be carried with you easily. You could also give it as a gift to a child. Like Idioms, at first glance it is not what you think it is.

History:

"Don't throw away the baby with the bath water." The origin of the use of idioms began by Thomas Murner, in 1512. Murner thought that some tried to throw away good ideas, while getting rid of some bad ideas at the same time appeared to be not a productive process. Tossing the baby out with the dirty bath water became the saying for this thought process.

The idiom in the previous paragraph became popular in the 1500's. Water was a limited commodity to families for bathing, so families would share the same bath water, by taking their turn bathing. The head of the house would bath first, then the men in the house, followed by the woman of the house, next the other women, then children and finally the baby. This is opposite of how babies are treated today, they would probably be bathed first in the fresh clean water, being fearful that they would catch some disease. When this idiom began, the baby being the last to bathe, the family wanted to make sure that the last bather, being the baby; the family did not want to make a mistake to throw out the baby in the dirty water. Therefore, "don't throw away the baby with the bath water."

Idioms are a twist of our English language that have hidden meaning in the phrases. All cultures have idioms that relate to their customs and cultures. Idioms are interesting, even though you understand the words used; the meaning of what they are trying to say can be a mystery. Idioms are hard to understand, but fun to use in conversations to see others response as they try to figure out what you are trying to say.

Let us look at some of these fun idioms and look at what they mean. One that comes to mind is, "when pigs fly." Everyone knows that pigs cannot fly. This saying originated in Germany or Scotland. Of course, pigs do not fly there either, but this phrase is used when the situation has an impossible solution.

Another common idiom is to "turn a blind eye" to a situation. The saying means that the person refuses to acknowledge the truth. This phrase originated by a British Admiral Horatio Nelson. In 1801 Admiral, Nelson led an attack with Admiral Sir Hyde Parker in the Battle of Copenhagen. Admiral Nelson was blind in one eye. At times signals given to him were with a flag, telling him to advance or retreat with the troops. Occasionally when Admiral Nelson had a differing opinion then Admiral Parker, he would put the telescope up to his blind eye and then push on with his plan. Since he used his blind eye to look in the telescope, this phrase came to life.

"Feeling under the weather," is a popular idiom. When sailors were feeling sick, they would go under the deck to the bow of the boat, hoping to feel better. This position in the boat had less motion and was out of the weather. This location on the boat began to become a place to rest and feel better from one's illness. Thus, "feeling under the weather."

Another popular idiom is when one, "beats around the bush." When someone wants to avoid a point and not tell someone what happened, beating around the bush is used. Children and youth might use this tactic when they do not want to tell their parents the truth about something that happened. Adults may use this in the workplace if they think confessing the truth might get them fired. The first origin of this phrase was when British hunters were hunting birds; they would shake the bush to capture the birds hiding in the bush.

If you "read someone the riot act," this idiom came from a real riot in Britain, during the 18th century. During the 1714 riots, King George I, and the government passed a Riot Act. The Kingdom and government were fearful of rioters overthrowing him, that the law passed to control unruly groups of people. Groups of 12 or more considered a riot, and the authorities would some to take care of the crowds. After passing this law, the use of this phrase when someone was acting unruly. Parents or law enforcement would say they were going to "read them the riot act," so they knew what they were doing was wrong and inappropriate.

"Spilling the beans," is not a good thing, it means that you let a secret slip, telling everyone the surprise before it is time. This idiom believed to be part of the ancient Greek voting method. Greek voters would use beans to cast their vote in a closed concealed container. A white bean to a voter cast a yes vote, and black or brown beans cast a no vote. If the container of beans spilled, the content revealed, disclose the secret ballot before it is time.

The idiom, "it costs an arm and a leg," believed to come from painters in the 18th century. When painters enlisted models for painting portraits, they would pay the model from their waist up. Painting a bust of a person was more affordable than completing a full model. The painter would pay more if they painted the entire person, so the cost would be higher. Therefore, the phrase, "costing an arm and a leg," became a saying when items were costing more than one thinks it should cost.

In the 1930's the poet Ogden Nash used the saying, "life is a piece of cake," in his book, "Primrose Path," his idiom was to let his reader know that life was easy for his characters. There are similar saying using food, like, "it's easy as pie," which also means that the task is easy to complete. If someone is the "apple of one's eye," it means that they have fond feelings towards another person. Another food idiom is the saying she has "a bun in the oven," which means someone is expecting a child. We may hear a few idioms in daily conversations but not often. Idioms are not literal meanings within the sentences, rather it creatives a colorful visual to express a concept or idea to the hearer or reader, with an underlying meaning, principle, or value. Just a lively way to express ones thoughts.

Activities:
- Finish a list of Idioms. (See next page)

FINISH THE IDIOMS AND DISCUSS THEIR MEANINGS.

1. 'The best of both _____.

2. 'Speak of the _____.

3. 'See eye to _____.

4. 'Once in a blue _____.

5 Let the cat out of _____ _____.

6. To kill two birds with _____.

7. To cut _____.

8. 'To add insult to _____.

9. 'You can't judge a book by _____.

10. 'Break a _____.

11. 'To hit the nail on the _____.

12. 'A blessing in _____.

13. 'Call it a _____.

14. 'Let someone off the _____.

15. 'No pain no _____.

16. 'Bite the _____.

17. 'Getting a taste of your own _____.

18. 'Giving someone the cold _____.

19. 'This is the last _____.

20. 'The elephant in the _____..

21. Stealing someone's _____.

22. Straight from the horse's _____.

IDIOMS ANSWERS

1. 'The best of both worlds'– means you can enjoy two different opportunities at the same time.

2. 'Speak of the devil' –this means that the person you are just talking about appears at that moment.

3. 'See eye to eye'– this means agreeing with someone.

4. 'Once in a blue moon'– an event that happens infrequently.

5. 'Let the cat out of the bag'– to accidentally reveal a secret.

6. 'To kill two birds with one stone'– to solve two problems at once.

7 'To cut corners'– to do something badly or cheaply.

8.'To add insult to injury – to make a situation worse.

9. 'You can't judge a book by its cover'– to not judge someone or something based solely on appearance.

10. 'Break a leg' –means 'good luck' (often said to actors before they go on stage).

11 'To hit the nail on the head' –to describe exactly what is causing a situation or problem.

12. 'A blessing in disguise' –A misfortune that eventually results in something good happening later.

13. 'Call it a day' –Stop working on something

14. 'Let someone off the hook' –To release a caught offender rather than punish him.

15. 'No pain no gain' –You must work hard for something you want.

16. 'Bite the bullet' –Decide to do something unpleasant that you have avoiding doing.

17. 'Getting a taste of your own medicine' –You will be treated the same unpleasant way you have treated others.

18. 'Giving someone the cold shoulder' –To ignore someone.

19. 'The last straw' –The final source of irritation causing someone to lose patience.

20. 'The elephant in the room' –A matter or problem that is obvious of great importance but that is not discussed openly.

21. 'Stealing someone's thunder' –Taking credit for someone else achievements.

MAY

Sock Hop

Food:
- Hamburgers, hot dogs, French fries, onion rings, milk shakes, popcorn in red and white containers.

Decorations:
- Checkerboard tablecloth, pink and/or turquoise plates, cups, and silverware.

Crafts:
- Poodle skirts
- How to make an ice cream soda craft. Get a Coke shaped glasses for each person. Get straws, pink, and white carnations (enough for every person to have 5-6 carnations/glass), and artificial cherries. In the coke glass, fill it with white tissue paper. Next, add the carnations to look like ice cream, add a straw in each glass. Finally glue an artificial cherry on top. Completed you have an Ice Cream Soda for each person to carry home. Then used them to decorate the table for the day.
- Cut patterns of eyeglasses out of cardboard or construction paper. Have a variety of poster board colors for participants to use to trace around the eyeglass patterns onto the poster board. Get stickers, stencil, markers, or paint for the participant to designs their glasses. After decorating, use Popsicle sticks or skewers to make a holder for the eyeglass frames.

History:

Sock Hops gained popularity in the 1940's and 50's as students headed to their school gyms for a fun night of dancing. As you walked into the gym, you would see it decorated with bubblegum pink, and teal - streamer, cups, plates and silverware, and black and white checkerboard tablecloths. The music would be the Rock and Roll songs like played on a jukebox. Most of the dance music came from the vinyl 45 rpm records played by a disc jockey. The name Sock Hop got its name because as students entered the gym, remove their shoes, so they would not mess up the gym floor – and the birth of the name – Sock Hop.

Sock Hops were very informal dances. The guys and girls did not spend lots of money to get the perfect formal dress and suit or tux for the evening. Rather these dances were very casual and did not only happen at night, but after school or before dinnertime. Guys casual dress was a white t-shirt and blue jeans, or if they wanted to dress to impress the girls, they would wear a button-down collar dress shirt, dress pants, penny loafers, and a black leather jacket.

Girls wore short sleeve sweaters with a removable peter pan collar, and a poodle skirt. The poodle skirts are a full skirt, with a synched elastic waist, decorated with a poodle applique. If you lay the skirt on the floor, it would make a full circle of black felt material. As their dance partner would twirl the girls around, their skirt would whirl around too. Some would help their full skirt stand out by wearing a several layer crinoline underneath. The poodle skirt is now the quintessential outfit for a 50's girl. Poodle skirts are worn for Halloween costumes still today. Not all parents approved of Sock

Hop dances. This new Rock and Roll music, thought to be "Devil music," accompanied by dance moves that involved shaking their hips in mixed company, was thought to be vulgar and unacceptable to more traditional, older folks. Youth loved it.

Today, a Sock Hop is often used as a fun theme for a party or school dance. We love to let our "hair down," and enjoy music from the 50's. Those who enjoyed Sock Hops growing up love to reminisce about their dance, decorations and boyfriend or girlfriend back in the days.

Activities:

- Puzzle with Sock Hop words.
- Guess that song Bingo with Rock and Roll Songs.
  Make bingo cards at this site:
  https://wordmint.com/pages/landing/bingo?headline=Bingo+Card+Creator&_puzzle_type=Bingo&bing_loc_physical_ms=87097&msclkid=e66a508918cf185758070f5369f26955&utm_source=bing&utm_medium=cpc&utm_campaign=bing.wordmint.bingo.phrase&utm_term=create%20your%20own%20bingo&utm_content=phrase.bingo_creator

SOCK HOP WORDS PUZZLE

```
R S A H R L K S W F V K E B K
D B R F U O Q I C A K F I N W
M O G E L H C K F T R I I K K
K B I V G A A K H X G P F I F
E B J P P R Y I A W D N D G S
A Y P Q W E U L J N W L U E P
C S P E N N Y B A S D C I O T
P O O D L E S K I R T R N V S
H C K Q I I C L K E F Y O I N
S K L E F A C K B F T I C L J
N S D I L Y I N G A P O J Y L
S T S B R N O Q I O E N F S S
V Z U Z A P P L P L D O F P X
C F F L Q K S M A E R C E C I
B S S U J U S M Q A B K K Q V
```

BLACK AND PINK
BOBBY SOCKS
BURGERS
COKE
FRIES
ICE CREAM
LOAFERS
PENNY
PONYTAILS
POODLE SKIRT
ROCK AND ROLL

Kermit the Frog Birthday Anniversary -May 9

Food:

- Make green iced cupcakes, use marshmallows for eyes and an edible black marker for the center eyeballs.

- Green Apples cut marshmallows in half and use them for eyes. Put black on with edible marker. You can cut apple wedges for his collar.

- Pigs in a blanket in honor of Ms. Piggy

Crafts:

- Clay pot frogs. Purchase a small clay flower-pot for each participant. Turn the pot upside down, paint the outside , and bottom green. Out of green foam sheets, cut frog feet and ovals for eyes. In the center of the green ovals, glue a google eye. After the paint dries, glue the ovals on one side of the clay pot. Glue the feet on the bottom of the pot. (See pattern below.) Use larger clay pots to decorate your garden.

- Make a frog or pig sock puppet. View videos on "How to make sock puppets."

History:

In 1955, a puppeteer, Jim Henson introduced one of the most beloved puppets to the stage - Kermit the Frog. Kermit was created by Jim, using his mother's worn-out turquoise coat, and two half-ping pong balls for eyes. Initially, this famous puppet was a lizard-like creature with an olive pointed collar. This collar helped to cover up the seam on the neck of the puppet. Thin wire were attached to the hands to animated the puppet to help Kermit come alive.

The Kermit puppet made its debut in 1955 on a TV show call, Sam and Friends, in Washington, D.C. Henson's popularity did not become famous until 1969, when he appeared on Sesame Street. The original name of Kermit was Kermit Scott, after Jim Henson's childhood friend, but for some reason Henson denied this fact by saying he just liked the name. Joy DiMenna, Kermit Scott's sister, said her dad's obituary said that Kermit was named after their father.

Sesame Street became a sensation around the world. Kermit's name was different in the other countries, but it was the same frog character. Another character, Miss Piggy, took the world by storm too, as Kermit's soon to be girlfriend. Miss Piggy puppet was created in 1974, for her TV appearance on Albert and the TJB show. Bonnie Erickson created this bigger than life character, and it surprisingly resembled the creator's face.

Kermit and Miss Piggy did not meet until 1976, while developing "The Muppet Show." Miss Piggy was always proclaiming that she had "love at first sight," for her frog friend Kermit. In 1978, cleaver Miss Piggy tried to trick Kermit into marriage. During her "sketch" for the show, Miss Piggy planned a mock wedding as part of the show. Little did Kermit know, Miss Piggy replaced the fake marriage license, and Minister for a real ones. Before the "I do's" were exchanged, the skit went wild, and no vows were exchanged. Miss Piggy was disappointed but Kermit was relieved.

It was not until the next year, while appearing on the Johnny Carson Show, that Miss Piggy tried to trick Kermit into another marriage proposal, but that one did not stick either. Years of trying to trap Kermit into marriage, it was not until 1984, in the "The Muppets Take Manhattan," when the two finally tied the knot. Kermit, saying that the minister was not an official minister, protested this marriage and the two remained single. Kermit still protests that all marriages on stage are just acting for the show, and not official. Miss Piggy still maintainss that she had a real minister and the backing of the puppet creator Jim Henson when the two were married. As a public display of the "break-up," in 1990 on "The Today Show," and the pair broke up once again. *People* Magazine also ran a story claiming that the couple have divorced. But once again, in 1993, the couple slipped on CNN and say that they were living together.

An exclusive in 1993 with Larry King, Kermit declared that he would never get married again. A year later, on "Good Morning Texas," Kermit denied any relationship with Miss Piggy. This on again, off again, relationship with these two-character ended with Miss Piggy declaring on their fiftieth Anniversary show, that they will always be married in their hearts.

This tumultuous relationship still played out in the Walt Disney Studios Motion Pictures. In 2011, Kermit lived in LA and Miss Piggy lived in Paris. In the tear-jerking episode, Kermit became vulnerable and almost told Miss Piggy that he loved her.

However, in 2014, the couple was making wedding plans once again, and Miss Piggy sported a diamond ring. But in 2015, the couple officially split up. Three years later the split remained, even though they care about each other in special ways, they are not good as a couple. In "The Muppets," Kermit made headlines for dating a different pig named Denise, but that relationship broke up after the first season.

It looks like Kermit the Frog, might have commitment issues, and should remain single instead of tugging at fellow puppets heartstrings.

Activities:

● Find Kermit's Friends word search.

HISTORY OF KERMIT AND FRIENDS PUZZLE

```
O M E K T A V P E S R O R A N
K E R M I T N A S E A Z E T J
D A D F E O G I T U C N K N Y
T M O M A L M O M O Q O A I V
I Q G N E Z O A S A L G E D X
B L D G J C R G Q G L F R W E
O K H Y S Q J Y F D O J B A Y
M S P R Q T F N B R T Q N L N
C R F I W E D Y E N O H H T J
Y G G I P C H E F O J D K E U
B J O X C E Y Y W L U U L R L
Q E T Z S O X I A U T F I A Y
F H A B Z I R K F M S B I G W
E Q X R W I Q N S L B Y S T O
N Z A R R C R F T O M P N Z G
```

ANIMAL	BEAR	BREAKER
CHEF	DOG	EAGLE
GONZO	HONEYDEW	KERMIT
MISS	PIGGY	RAT

May 14th – Chicken Dance Day

Food:

Chicken wings with different sauces. Deviled eggs or hard-boiled eggs.

Crafts:

- A chicken crafts. You can use buttons or different colors of dried beans, peas, rice, to fill in the feathers. Put it on foam core board.
  https://www.pinterest.com/pin/772578511065498632/
- Chicken potholder with pattern. Hand sewn.
  https://www.pinterest.com/pin/92112754858191583/

History:

If you have ever been to a wedding you are familiar with a fun party song and dance, "The Chicken Dance." Those who are not usually on the dance floor feels comfortable getting up on the floor to flap their arms like wings and twisting their torso to the music. This fun song and dance were a brainchild of an accordion player Werner Thomas from Davos, Switzerland, in the 1950's. This song was originally called Der Ententanz, which means Duck Dance, later known as Chicken Dance and Dance Little Bird. This song migrated to the United States in the 1950's, a couple of years after Stanley Mills from New York acquired publishing rights to this song.

This song did not just stay in Switzerland and the United States, Rob Grant and Doug Naylor wrote fun lyrics and new music as Britain satirical comedy enjoyed doing the Chicken Dance. Henry Hadaway, from the United Kingdom came on board with this fun music and dance in 1981. Hadaway produced a new version of the Chicken Dance as an instrumental tune. A United Kingdom group, the Tweets, made the "The Birdie Song" popular rising to the number two spot the fall of that year.

If you are not familiar with the "Chicken Dance," the movements are simple. As the song begins you use your hands to form duck "beaks." Four quacks with your hands, then move to placing your hands under your arm pits to make bird wings, flapping four times.

Next you twist your body also four times while bending your knees, ending with clapping your hands four times. The music continues as you as you go through these moves four times. The interlude of the music you lock one arms with your partner and skip in a circle. You will recognize the music beginning again for your duck "beaks" and you repeat the process several times until the music ends. Lots of fun and great exercise as everyone smile and laughs – try it. The according player may add to the fun by speeding up the music as the song goes on.

So where did this idea of a Chicken Dance come from? Is it about the joy of raising chickens? Are chickens joyful? No recorded evidence that chickens dance, unless you count the courtship ritual that is performed by roosters as he circles a hen that he wants to breed with. Hens are heard clucking and cackling when they are about to lay eggs, and everyone is happy to have the eggs in the nest, whether it's to eat for breakfast or to hatch another chick. Chickens may have appeared happy to their owners, which might have given Werner Thomas, from Switzerland, the idea for the Chicken Dance. So try it, it is great exercise and a lot of fun.

Activities:
    *Do the Chicken Dance with group.

History Of Redheads

Food:
- Red velvet cake or cupcakes,

Crafts:
- Paint a picture of a fox – they have red hair. Get a frame to put the picture in.

History:

Redhead, ginger, or carrot top might be what you are called by friends or family, whether you like it or not, if you have red hair. Redheads often get lots of attention due to their noticeable hair color. Many popular redheads like Lucy Ball, Carol Burnett, or Pippy Longstocking, have made red hair a popular. Sometimes redheads do not like all the attention, because it does not feel like a positive reaction to their hair color, while others love the attention they get for having red hair.

Redheads were part of ancient times too. Believe it or not, red hair was seen in several of Pharaohs Egyptian mummies. Ramesses II, the most powerful Pharaoh, who ruled from 1303 BC to 1213 BC, had ginger hair. Ramesses the Great was what his community called him.

Redheads were also part of Greek literature in 500 BC. A Greek poet, Xenophanes, developed gods in their own image with blue eyes and red hair. In 400 BC, the nation of Budnik had a powerful nation of redheads. Ancient Greeks admired people with red hair. They were associated with honor and courage. In Greek mythology, some of the most beautiful women were the ones with red hair. The goddess of love, beauty, sexuality, and fertility was beloved Aphrodite, adorned red hair. Another beautiful famous redhead woman was Cleopatra.

Although many famous, beloved individuals were redheads, some feel that redheads are unlucky or bring bad luck. Actors in Greek and Roman times depicted slaves wore red hair wigs. Some myths thought that redheads would turn into vampires upon death. Egyptians felt that ginger hair individuals were bad luck and to get rid of the bad events from occurring, was to sacrifice the redhead. The sacrificial methods would usually be to bury them alive.

The treatment of ginger haired individuals varied across cultural lines, and fortunately, today theses drastic treatments and beliefs do not continue. Some people like to tease people with red hair, but some teasing might be just a way to flirt with them or a jealous streak because they would like red hair too. Whether in Ancient times or today, the beautiful red hair individuals gain lots of attention everywhere they go.

If you are a ginger hair person, you might want to know some interesting facts about being a ginger. Only two percent of people around the world are redheads and the greatest numbers of them are in Scotland, which has 13%, and the second highest numbers you will find in Ireland with 10% of their population sporting red hair.

Most redheads have either brown, hazel, or green eyes, but if you see a redhead with blue eyes, they are rare - only point seventeen percent have this combination.

In the Netherlands Bart Rouwenhorst wanted to get 15 redhead models, so he placed an advertisement requesting redheads. He had 150 individuals show up to try out for the ad, so he had a lottery drawing for the ad models. This event began The Redhead Days festival, which is the largest international event highlighting natural redheads. The funny part of this festival was that a blonde-haired person started it.

Redheads must be careful when they get in the sun, because they are more sensitive to getting sun burnt and are more sensitive to pain. Because of this sensitivity, they have a higher risk of cancer. An interesting twist is that ginger men have a 54% lower risk of developing prostate cancer compared to men with blonde-hair or brunette hair. If redheads need surgery, they need more anesthesia to put them to sleep for the surgery than those with blonde or brown hair.

Ginger heads have 90,000 strands of hair but the strands are thicker compared to the 110,000 strands for blondes and 140,000 strands for brunettes. The good thing is that they do not go gray. Their hair changes as they age from red, to blonde, and then white hair, as the pigment fades.

The rumors of redhead population decreasing in our world is a myth. In fact, 30% of ads we see on TV features people with ginger hair. Some interesting facts is that redheads produce more vitamin D in a shorter time than other hair colors. For a couple to have a red-haired child, both mother and father must have the red hair gene. Another trait for gingers is that they often are left-handed. Research shows that recessive traits usually come in pairs. Red hair is a recessive trait and being left-handed is a recessive trait, when they join in a baby the result is a left-handed redhead individual.

Redheads should celebrate the fact that they have beautiful ginger colored hair and through a party on May 26, World Redhead Day and then do not forget to celebrate again November 5 for National Love Your Red Hair Day. Make sure you get lots of food because 140 million redheads worldwide might just show up.

Activities:
- Guess the famous redheads as a group. See quiz sheet on next page. This will encourage discussion when remembering the redheads and what they did as a career.

FAMOUS REDHEADS QUIZ

1. A comedian who played in a show with Ricky Ricardo?   Lucille Ball

2. The man known as the Crocodile Hunter? - Steve Irwin

3. A British politician, army officer, writer, and UK Prime Minister? Winston Churchill

4. Comedian who pulled her ear at the end of her shows to tell her mom she loved her?   Carol Burnette

5. British Prince? - Prince Harry

6. He played Opie on the Andy Griffith Show as a child.   Ron Howard

7. Late night host of a talk show?   Conan O'Brien

8. Highest British leader who likes to wear hats and white gloves? Elizabeth I

9. Female country singer and comedian who was in a sitcom as a divorced mom living next door to her ex and new wife?   Reba McEntire

10. A wild comedian whose shows include him smashing foods like watermelons on stage. Carrot Top

11. An Australian-American actress who played in "Days of Thunder" with Tom Cruise? Nicole Kidman

12. One of the women on "The View"

13. First President of the United States?   George Washington

14. Cook, author, blogger, and photographer. Also has her own TV cooking show. Reed Drummond

15. American actor, comedian, radio personality, and professional wrestler? Danny Bagaduce.

Creation of Popeye Cartoon

Food:

- Wimpy hamburger sliders, and spinach salad with "Olive Oyl" dressing.

Craft:

- Get sailor hats for each participant and have them decorate their hat.

- Paint wooden boats. They can be ordered from craft magazines or pick them up   in craft stores. You also will need acrylic paint in a variety of colors. Pictures of his boat are different colors, red, brown, yellow, and blue. You will need paint brushes. Let them create their boat to their choosing.

History:

A favorite cartoon to many children in 1929 was Popeye the Sailor Man.   Elzie Crisler Segar, a cartoonist from Chester, Illinois, modeled this character from a person in her hometown, Mr. Rocky Fiegel. Olive Oyl was based on Dora Pascal, another local person in town. This television cartoon was first a daily newspaper comic strip. The Daily King, a worldwide syndicate paper, distributes about 5,000 newspapers worldwide, taking Popeye the Sailor Man, around the world.

In 1929, Thimble Theater, put these comic strip characters into animated television show. The wisecracking, hot tempered sailor, Popeye, was quick to start fights with Brutus, his competition for his girlfriend Olive Oyl. His nemesis Brutus was also picking fights with Popeye, to get the girl. When this happened, Popeye was known to pull out a can of spinach from his shirt, and gain strength to win the fight with Brutus. Popeye's can of spinach was his secret weapon for extra strength when other situations would arise too. Popeye's go to vegetable, made the sales of spinach increase to about one third more in sales during the height of his popularity.

Later, "Famous Studios," renamed to Paramount Cartoon Studios, showed Popeye the Sailor Man cartoon, from 1942 to 1957. These cartoons were streamlined drawings because of the low budget, and to simplify the cartoon for television. The simplified drawings allowed for the cartoonist to produce 220 made-for-television cartoons, in only two short years. This may seem like a long time, but the 231 theatrical cartoons took 24 years to produce for the stage.

Although World War II was over, the Navy uniform dress, remained the outfit for Popeye. Olive Oyl was dressed very matronly, in a long black skirt with a red turtleneck, and huge boot like shoes. Her hair was mid 40's style, flat to her head and pulled back in a bun/ponytail. Not a beauty queen for Popeye and Brutus to be fighting over, but she was a kindhearted person for sure.

In 1937, Parmont Studios employed Popeye in his first film with Betty Boop, called, Popeye the Sailor Man. Cities were so excited about this movie, that they erected a statue in Crystal City, Texas, to honor this cartoon characters, Popeye. Crisler Segar hometown of Chester, Illinois also erected a Popeye Statue, along with 14 other characters from this comic strip. As you stroll down State Street, in Chester, Illinois, you can find all of your favorite characters from the hamburger eating Wimpy, adorable baby Sweet Pea, and nemesis Brutus, to name a few.

Brutus or Bluto is the same characters, but his name was changed after the theatrical Popeye show ceased in 1957. The originally named "Bluto," was said to be the rights of Famous Studio, so they had to change the name. "Brutus" was the name change for this brute of a character, which made a smooth transition for television views.

A beloved character of the cartoon strip was Wimpy. Segar developed this character after the manager of Chester Opera House. This Illinois man, known as "Windy Bill," was kind and friendly man, known for his tall tales and his love for hamburgers. In the comic strip and television series, he was Popeye's soft-spoken friend who was the role of the "straight man." He was a romantic, intelligent but lazy man, with an insatiable hunger for hamburgers. His favorite line was "I will gladly pay you Tuesday, for a hamburger today." Being quite the scam artist, he always relied on the generosity of the cook for free food, but rarely receive the hamburgers he desired. Wimpy pretended to have high social status, he was quite the scam artist, mooching off whoever would oblige his wishes. He would even smoke the discarded cigars of others. Popeye continuously tried to reform Wimpy, but his laziness would not allow for a change in his ways.

Finally, is the baby, Swee' Pea. This baby boy was mailed to Popeye, and left on his doorstep, in the July 24, 1933 comic strip. Popeye adopts this boy and raises him as his son. His name came from an endearing term, Rocky Fiegel used to address people in his hometown.

A wonderful cast of characters have been enjoyed on television, by children and adults, since 1929. Even today, reruns of the Popeye cartoons, can be enjoyed by families. If you watched Popeye, what was your favorite character, and why?

Activities:

- Try your hand at drawing Popeye. Step by step instructions can be printed off online at
https://dragoart.com/tut/how-to-draw-popeye-easy-15557

- Use the letters of each of the characters names and write adjectives describing that character. e.g., P = polite, O = outgoing etc. You can use each name, Popeye, Olive Oyl, Swee'Pea, Wimpy, and Brutus, and do the same activity with their names.

POPEYE ACROSTIC ACTIVITY

P

O

P

E

Y

E

POPEYE'S FRIENDS

O

Y

L

W

H

I

M

P

Y

B

R

U

T

U

S

JUNE

Drive-in Movies

Food:
- Concession food like popcorn in red and white containers, candy, hot dogs, hamburgers

Crafts:
- Get a box for each participant. Have them decorate the boxes like a car for the "Drive In" movie.
- Paint a picture with watercolors of a Drive-In Movie theater.

History:

Who would have thought a northern cooler weather state would be the first to have drive-ins movie theaters. On June 6, 1933, Richard Hollingshead from New Jersey got this wonderful idea to show a movie on a large screen outside. His idea came to him when he thought about how uncomfortable movie theater seats were to sit in while watching a 1 1/2 -to-2-hour movie. He tried out his idea at home for his mom, allowing her to bring his other sibling in a more comfortable seating arrangement for everyone. Kids could sit on the grass or fall asleep if they got tired in the back seat of the car. The Drive-In movie allowed everyone regardless of how noisy the children were.

Drive-In Theaters took off, growing to more and more around New Jersey and other states around the country. This idea did not only remain in the United States but became an internationally phenomenon. The 1950's and 1960's with the baby boomer, Drive-In's were a great way to have a date or family outing for 20 years.

The only pitfall of the Drive-In was the weather. Warm weather was a necessary, the snow, ice or sleet, would not be fun at the Drive-In. However, fall dates to the Drive-In showed couples snuggled up together, under blankets to keep warm. A great way to get close to your favorite guy or girl and watch your favorite movie.

The economic effect of smaller cars and prices of maintaining your car, coupled with the invention of the VCU took families out of the Drive-In for the convenience of their own homes. Renting or purchasing a movie for family viewing made a more affordable way to enjoy a movie. In addition, families could provide their own popcorn or snack, and have easy access to the bathroom. Slowly the Drive-In movies dwindled until there are only a few locations across the United States. There are only 300 Drive-Ins in operation. You would find them in Ohio, New York, Pennsylvania, and Virginia. No matter how many remain in the United States, the nostalgic memories of piling into a car with family or friends to watch a movie is a fun childhood memory.

Activities:
- Watch an old movie.
- Word scramble of old movies.

DRIVE-IN MOVIE WORD SCRAMBLE PUZZLE

GENO TIWH HET DNWI   _ _ _ _ _   _ _ _ _   _ _ _   _ _ _ _ _

                 19   7

NIISNGG NI HET NIAR   _ _ _ _ _ _ _ _   _ _   _ _ _   _ _ _ _ _

                                                 5

YM RAFI LYAD   _ _   _ _ _ _   _ _ _ _

                 8   17

SIT A LUERFWODN FELI   _ _   _   _ _ _ _ _ _ _ _ _   _ _ _ _

                                    1   18

SOCGORE   _ _ _ _ _ _ _

                 2

MYAR SIPPOPN   _ _ _ _   _ _ _ _ _ _ _

                 14   3

ESEAGR   _ _ _ _ _ _ _

               12

VAIV SAL GAESV   _ _ _ _   _ _ _   _ _ _ _

                4 10   16

KAMHOLOA   _ _ _ _ _ _ _ _

                   9

TEWS DIES SYTRO   _ _ _ _   _ _ _ _   _ _ _ _ _

                   11   15

TEH RISB   _ _ _   _ _ _ _

               6

IWTEH MHRSCITSA   _ _ _ _ _   _ _ _ _ _ _ _ _ _

                                 13

_ _ _ _ _   _ _   _ _ _ _ _ _   _ _ _   _ _ _ .

1 2 3 4 5   6 7   8 9 10 11 12 13   14 15 16   17 18 19

Garfield the Cat Day is June 19th

Collect a variety of Garfield cartoons for several weeks and display them on orange and black construction paper around the room. You can also print off photos of Garfield in different positions to display too, or for the group to color ahead of time.

Food:
- You can serve Garfield's favorite food – Lasagna or if you want something lighter as a snack you could serve Cheese-It's, Cheetos, and Orange soda.

Craft:
- Copy some photos of Garfield to color or paint.

History:

An American comic strip Artist and creator, Jim Davis, brought everyone's favorite tabby cat Garfield to life in 1976. Davis created this lazy orange and black cat with an insatiable appetite, especially for lasagna. Garfield comic strip became a National Syndication in 1978, featuring Garfield, his owner, Jon Arbuckle, and Odie, Jon's dog. Their popularity grew and in 2013 it was syndicated in roughly 2,580 newspapers and journals and holds the Guinness World Record for being the most syndicated comic strip series.

Garfield is like many of us, - hating Mondays, loves to eat, likes being lazy, enjoys coffee, and hates dieting. Garfield also has the tendency to manipulate people, in shroud ways, to get what he wants.

Davis' choice of drawing a cat comic was because he saw that the dog comics were doing well in the comic strips, but there was not any successful cat comics. He also felt the 25 cats on the farm where he grew up, gave him several characteristics and antics he observed growing up, gave him a lot of material for his cat Garfield comic.

Garfield was named and characterized after Jim Davis, grouchy, disagreeable grandfather, James A. Garfield Davis. These characteristics can be seen when Garfield pushes Odie off the counter or eats all the lasagna leaving nothing for the others.

Garfield's owner, Jon Arbuckle, came from a 1950's coffee commercial character who had childish actions. Some of his childish ways were part of Jon's persona. For example, he would often dress in a mis-matched outfit to go on dates, which ended in a one date cycle for Jon, until he met Dr. Liz Wilson. She liked Jon and overlooked his mismatched dressing and childish antics. This was when Jon's girlfriend Liz, became part of the comic strip.

On August 8, 1978, Jon Arbuckle's yellow beagle dog Odie became part of the cartoon strip. Odie was Davis' roommates' dog who later was given to Davis. Odie became Jon's other pet in the cartoon strip. Garfield loves to bully Odie and he was portrayed as a dumb, simple dog in most of the cartoon strips, but occasionally his response to Garfield antics was extremely clever. This twist was the revenge some wanted to see for Odie in the Garfield strip.

Most of the interaction in this comic strip was between Garfield, Jon and Odie, but on June 26, 1979, Dr. Elizabeth "Liz" Wilson appeared in her first Garfield comic. Liz was Garfield's veterinarian who had a crush on Jon for quite some time. One would think that her stoic, straight face persona was quite a contrast to Jon's childish quirky persona. Jon attempted to date her but was not successful until June 20 to July 29, 2006. Liz finally proclaimed her love to Jon, and she became the fourth character in the comic strip.

Garfield not only shows up in comic strips, but on T.V. Cartoons shows, featured in children's books, movies, and toy store stuffed animals. This grouchy cat can be seen on office desks in the Garfield daily desk calendars. Jon proposed marriage to Liz, and as a veterinarian she began nagging Garfield to lose weight and eat healthier. Although she nags him about eating right, she brings Garfield's favorite foods for him to enjoy.

On April 19, 2019 Garfield's teddy bear and best friend, Pooky, showed up in the comic strips. Although he was stuffed in a drawer, he would often bring him out for a hug or conversation with his friend. Over the years Pooky was wearing out, and he even lost one of his eyes. Garfield love for his friend brought him to asked for an eye for Pooky for Christmas. We all need a good friend in life like Pooky.

Activities:

- Copy some photos of Garfield and try to draw him. You can google, "How to Draw Garfield the Cat," and there are step by step instructions. **https://www.wikihow.com/Draw-Garfield**

- Make cat cookies and decorate them with orange and black frosting.

- Google Garfield Trivia Questions

History and Invention of Eyewear

Food:

- Eyeglass frames = Sliced boiled eggs attached with string cheese. Kiwi circles connected with pretzel sticks. You could have cupcakes with candy or icing eyes.

Crafts:

- Use clay to form eyeglass frames. When the clay dries, paint them. The place where glass goes in the frame, you could put small photos of their family or friends.

- Use eyeglass pattern and trace them on cardboard. Decorate the frames with paint, markers, sequins, buttons, pearls or beads. (pattern on page 57)

History:

As we look around the room, we might see that many in the room have something in common - we wear glasses. Glasses today not only help us see the fine print, or complete a task, it also helps us to make a fashion statement.

The maker of the first pair of glasses is unknown, but the first group of inventors who discovered that pieces of glass could enhance one's ability to see were the Romans. The pieces of glass were not put together to wear on one's face to see better until the 13th century by an Italian named Salvino D'Armati. Later discovered that eyeglasses appeared in Pisa, Italy in the 1200's, with two convex-shaped magnifying circles put on two circular frames connected over the nose to help people see better.

In 1266, an Englishman Roger Bacon, a Franciscan Friar, wrote the principles of corrective lenses. Although Bacon knew the principles of seeing better with pieces of glass, he did not ever put this information together in a pair of eyeglasses. It took 1000 years before a mathematician named Alhazen, who put this knowledge together, becoming the "Father of Modern Optics."

In the beginning, eyeglasses frames were wood or leather, or occasionally animal horns were used. During the Renaissance age, glass blowers made lenses of various thicknesses for different eye correction needs. Italian creations of eyeglasses grew, but mainly purchased by the wealthy due to the cost of the blown glass. As blown glass became the main testing tool, you saw an increase in popularity of eyeglass wears in Italy and throughout Europe.

This process did not progress until 1700's when Benjamin Martin invented the hands-free eyeglass frame. The new frame attached in the center of one's face, with two stems, that would fasten behind the ears. Martin also created a more accurate, lightweight thinner lens, with a more durable frame. Martin's inventions made wearing his frame more comfortable and a longer lasting frame for children.

Many are surprised the Benjamin Franklin did not invent eyeglasses, but he was famous for inventing bi-focal lens. This eyewear allows the wearer to see close for reading and sewing, as well as seeing the signs ahead for driving. This invention allows us to wear one pair of glasses for both tasks, instead of having to change from close tasks too far away tasks by just moving one's head. This process changes from far away sight called near-sighted and close-up assistance to see called far-sighted vision.

As we go through the ages and look at styles of eyeglasses, we see several different styles. You might remember the scissor spectacles. They were small glasses that could be stored easily in your pocket for easy access. Women began to change their looks by choosing different frames around their eyeglasses. In the 1900's Rimless, glasses would sit on men's noses for reading, and Monocles were used but it did not allow for a hands-free reading. In the 1920 and 1930's, the rounded frames became popularity. We saw these frames in silent movies. In the 40 and 50's, playful frames became popular. Bright color, plastic frames, and the birth of the "Cat Eye Frame." Marilyn Monroe and Audrey Hepburn made these frames popularity.

In the 1960's and 1970's, eyeglasses became large and over-sized. These frames brought attention to the wearer who wanted to be flashy and noticed. In the 80 and 90's, the fashion turned to retro looks, bringing back the Cat Eye frames, and brow lined accented frames. A variety of looks was the fashion. Today, all types of frames our seen-on faces as we go about our day. All styles are popular for men and women today. From Cat eye frames, round, oval, square, to over-sized bright color frames, are all fashionable looks. What is your favorite look?

Eyewear not only helps us to see better, but it has also become a fashion statement, and a fun way to accent ones' outfit and change one's look day after day.

Activities:

- Use the acronym **E Y E G L A S S E S** and think of fun adjectives to describe different eyeglasses feelings when you wear different frames. Each letter will represent one word. (E.g. E = energetic, Y = youthful etc.)

USE THE ACRONYM OF EYEGLASSES TO DESCRIBE HOW GLASSES MAKE YOU FEEL

E

Y

E

G

L

A

S

S

E

S

National Waffle Iron Day

Food:
- Waffles, maple syrup, strawberries, blueberries, pineapple, whip cream and/or other syrups like blueberries, caramel, chopped nuts and ice cream.

Crafts:
- Purchase waffle paper from hobby store, Etsy, Castlehill crafts, scrapbook.com, or you could use corrugated cardboard. Purchase the paper in difference colors for the flowers and green for the leaves. If you use cardboard, paint them different colors before construction the flowers. Use flower patterns below. Cut out the shapes in the waffle paper and stack two on top of one another and attach to a piece of paper or 8 X 10 poster board. You could attach them to dowel rods as stems.

History:
In the 14th century, waffles got their start in Western Europe and the nations of Belgium, Netherlands and Luxembourg. This might be where the name, "Belgium Waffles," got its name. The first waffle iron had small intricate designs, made of metal. Pancake batter is put on the two metal plates and cooked over an open fire. The iron designs were usually a religious symbol like a cross, or a family coat of arms.

The Greeks of Athens were also thought to be the originators of waffle. Their flat cakes were also made by pressed batter between two metal plates and cooked over open fire. Another competitor of the waffle inventor was Cornelius Swarthout of Troy, New York. In 1869, he patented a stove-top waffle-maker. Although waffle irons existed since the 1300's, Swarthout updated the iron to have a handle and clasp to make it safer for the cook. In 1911 the birth of the electric waffle iron prototype was produced by General Electric, and in 1918 it became available for use by the public. The updated electric waffle iron gave us a quick and easy way to serve up breakfast.

The invention of the electric waffle iron, waffles became quite popular for breakfast and dessert treats. The most popular topping used is maple syrup, but soon strawberries and whipped cream grew in popularity. Waffles are now topped with blueberries or pineapples, for a healthy addition. For a dessert version one might add ice cream covered with blueberries, chocolate, or caramel syrup, topped with whipped cream.

Waffle irons were not just used to make waffles. In 1904 at the St. Louis Fair a new shell to hold ice cream was invented. The popular waffle cone which held a larger quantity of ice cream made its debut. Abe Doumar from Norfolk, Virginia created the waffle cone which is still enjoyed today by young and old alike.

The waffle iron did not stop with ice cream cones. Nike co-Founder Bill Bowerman, an Oregon Track Coach was trying to help his track stars have a better non-slip footing for his runners. He noticed his wife's waffle iron and thought it could provide the gripping surface he was looking for to use as the souls of the track shoes. After much experimentation, Bowerman designed the perfect track shoes in 1972 and called them "Moon Shoes." In 1974 they called his new invent, "Waffle Trainers." These waffle soul shoes, gave Nike their Blue Ribbon Start.

Whether you like waffles and syrup for breakfast, or waffles topped with fruit, ice cream, and whipped cream for dessert, they are always a favorite treat for many.

Activities:
- Waffle topping Scramble puzzle puzzle.

  Chocolate, strawberry, banana, caramel, whipped cream, chocolate chips, syrup, peanut butter, sprinkles, blueberries, maple, honey, ice cream, and cherry.

History of Carousels

Food:
- Carnival foods: corn dogs, popcorn, funnel cakes, candy apples, or caramel apples

Crafts:
- Solo cup, plastic, or plastic straws cut out carousel horse, (see pattern below), enough for each participant. Color with crayons or markers. After carousel horse is colored, cut out horse and glue it to a straw. Poke a hole in the center of an upside-down cup and stick the straw in cup and hot glue it to secure it. Decorate the cup as you desire.

History:

As you hear lively carnival music, it draws you to the carousel of horses going around and around, and up and down. The brightly colored horses are filled with children and parents going up and down, and round and round with big smiles on their faces. The breeze from the twirling carousel brushed across your face, as you waited for your turn on the carousel ride.

In 1845 the first carousel appeared at the fairs in Manhattan, New York. In 1850 the first merry go round, with dancing horses was patented in the United States. Carousels in the United States run clockwise. In Italy, Britain, and the United Kingdom they are called Merry-go-round and they turn counterclockwise.

The construction of carousels horses arranged to imitate galloping horses in a race around the platform is how the name galloper was used for this fun ride. Less common names for the merry-go-round are, jumper, horse about, and flying horses. Horses were used for all the people to ride, but later carousels began to have other animals to ride on like ostrich, tigers, zebras, pig, mythological creatures, and lions. They also have benches for older riders to sit and reminisce about younger years at the fair.

Merry-go-rounds started popping up all over Europe, in England, Germany, Italy, and France. Beautifully decorated horses racing up and down and around at the merry-go-round brought excitement to all the fair attenders. Children's eyes widened as they rushed to ride on their favorite horse or other animal.   Younger children might ride with their parent or grandparent on one of the decorative benches.

In the Silicon Valley California and in Santa Clara, California you can ride a two-story grand carousel. These grand carousels are two of the largest in the United States. An extra thrill is experienced by the riders on the second level of these carousels, allowing all the riders to enjoy the sights all around the fair as they ride around and around.

All ages enjoy the experience of the merry-go-round because it brings back grand
memories from their childhood. Merry-go-rounds are also safe for people of all ages who have outgrown the thrill of roller coasters and haunted houses. If you want to relive a childhood experience, hop on a carousel, and enjoy the thrill of the ride.

Activities:
- Use the letters of the word **C A R O U S E L** have the participants think up adjectives beginning with the letters in "carousel" You can do this activity as a group or individually.
- As each participant the following questions:
  Do you enjoy riding the carousel?
  What was your favorite thing to do at the fair?
  What was the most fun ride?
  What was their favorite fair food?
- Have a discussion with the group. Say the carousel goes around. What events or items have come back around in your lifetime? E.g., fashions, canning foods from the garden. etc.

History of Amelia Earhart

Food:

- Coffee, Tea, Soda, Peanuts, and pretzels. Airline foods.

Crafts:

- Purchase model airplanes for each participant for them to paint and decorate.

- Use the balsam airplane kits for each participant to assemble, and then fly. See whose airplane goes the farthest.

History:

On July 24, 1897, in Atchison, Kansas, an energetic, adventurous girl was born to Edwin and Amy Otis Earhart. Amelia Earhart was born into a wealthy family. Her father was a lawyer for Rock Island Railroad, which allowed her to attend a private school for her education. In 1909, Amelia and her younger sister, Muriel, moved to Des Moines, Iowa when the Railroad moved their father's job. During that time, they attended the Iowa State Fair, where Earhart first set eyes on the Wright Brothers airplane. This was not long after Orville, and Wilber Wright had made their first flight at Kitty Hawk, North Carolina.

After the move, their family was having difficulty because Earhart's father began drinking and causing turmoil in the Earhart household. Amy Earhart left her husband taking the girls with her to live with a friend in Springfield, Illinois. This family turmoil left an impression on Earhart, and a disdain for alcohol. The loss of her happy family and financial security, Amelia vowed not to follow her father's example.

Earhart graduated in Hyde Park School in Chicago, Illinois in 1915. The yearbook's superlative wrote, "the girl in brown who walked alone," Earhart had become a loner with all the events in her family. A year later Amelia received her grandmother's inheritance. She used the money to attend Ogontz School in Philadelphia. During her Christmas break, she went to Toronto, Canada where her sister was attending a private school.

While in Canada, Earhart observed soldiers who returned wounded from World War I and observed her first amputee surgery. This changed Earhart's focus and remained in Canada as a volunteer nurse in the veteran's hospital. Earhart remained there for 2 years, and then returned to live with her mother in Northampton, Massachusetts, while attending Columbia University. In 1919, her parents got back together, so she went to Los Angeles, California to join her parents.

The winter of 1920 was a pivotal year for Earhart when she attended her first air show. She was able to take her first plane ride, and as soon as she left the ground, she knew she had to fly. Flying lessons soon followed at the Kinner's airfield on Long Beach Boulevard, from Neta Snooks, a women pilot. A year later, 1921, Earhart was presented with her pilot license from National Aeronautics Association. Being determined to purchase her own plane, she worked as a file clerk, office assistant, photographer, and truck driver and was able to save enough to purchase her own plane. But there were trials for this expensive hobby.

Unfortunately, Earhart had to sell her plane in 1924 because her parents split again, and she purchased a car to drive her mother to Boston to be with her schoolteacher sister Muriel. Never giving up Earhart enrolled in Columbia University, in New York City, but soon ran out of money and had to return to Boston with her mother and sister. There Earhart worked as a social worker and joined the NAA so she could fly in her spare time.

Finally, four years later, in 1928, she was invited to join a crew flying across the Atlantic Earhart was bitten with the flying bug again. This flight was part of publicity of George Palmer Putnam, the editor of Charles Lindbergh's book, WE. His plan was to attract attention to readers making her the first female to fly alone across the Atlantic Ocean as "Lady Lindy." This event was in 1927, but Amelia was not impressed with this flight because she never touched the controls, she said that she was nothing more than "a sack of potatoes." Earhart was only chosen for this trip because of her flying experience, her education, and her attractive appearance.

Putnam saw Earhart as a good money-making scheme, so he became her manager setting up many speaking engagement, appearances, and tours. In 1931 he married her. He also set up interviews and public appearances, and even would describe his wife as a "puppet figure." To further her publicity and demonstrate her skill, he set up a tiny single-engine flight from Newfoundland, Canada to Ireland. In the Lockheed Electra plane. These trips and skills led to a solo flight on May 20-21 across the Atlantic, five years after the Lindbergh flight.

Earhart's energetic and successful career led her to become an advocate for women's rights and for commercial aviation for women. From 1931to 1937 Earhart set numerous records, from the fastest nonstop transcontinental flight, breaking her own speed records across several states, as well as becoming the first woman to fly across the Pacific from Hawaii to California solo. All these performances allowed her to collect numerous awards and honors all around the world.

On July 2, 1937, was one of the saddest days in history for the aviation community and the woman and girls who followed her success. Twenty-two days prior to her fortieth birthday Earhart set out to fly around the world. After logging 22,000 miles in the air, with her navigator, Fred Noonan, the two and their plane disappeared over the Pacific Ocean. They became missing between Lae, New Guinea, and Howland Island within the Pacific Ocean. The U.S. Navy performed a major search for the two and the plane for weeks, but the search was unsuccessful at recovering any part of the plane, Earhart, and Fred.

In 1997, as a tribute to Amelia Earhart, on 100 years after her birth, Linda Finch, retraced Earhart's flight successfully. This flight was called "World Flight 97," which was 26,000 total miles and took 73 days. Finch used the same type of plane as Earhart did, but it was modified with a Global Positioning System, increased gasoline capacity, and a modern communication system. Later Finch began a "You Can Soar education and motivational program in a variety of classrooms across the world to follow their dream of flying. There were 200,000 classrooms that shared Earhart's and Finch's love for flying to many woman and men across the world.

Activities:
- Fold paper, into airplanes. Get a Hula Hoop to see who can throw the paper airplane through the hoop. You can make teams to see who wins.

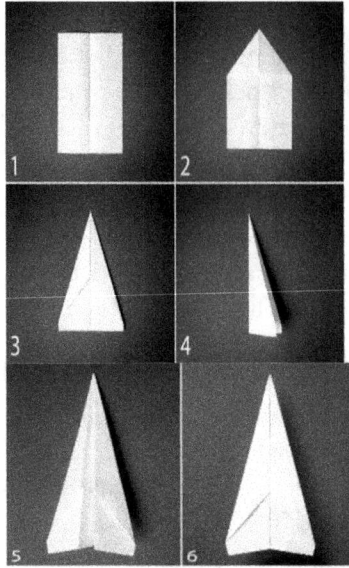

1. Fold the paper in half vertically.

2. Unfold the paper and fold each of the top corners into the center line.

3. Fold the top edges into the center line.

4. Fold the plane in half toward you.

5. Fold the wings down, matching the top edges up with the bottom edge of the body.

6. Add double stick tape to the inside of the body. The finished plane should look like this.

JULY

National Watch Day

Food:
- Round crackers, round slices of cheese, salami slices. (To look like round watches)

Crafts:
- Homemade Sundial. - Purchase sturdy white paper plates, pencils, and markers. On the back of the sturdy white paper plate, write the clock numbers, 1 -12, around the edge of the paper plate. Take the pencil and poke it through the center from the other side so that the pencil sticks straight up. Face the number 12 to the North to tell the time. Use the sun or a flashlight to test your sundial craft for the time.

History:
June 19th marks National Watch Day. The watch industry has been around for 500 years. As you look around you can see a variety of wrist watches worn by individuals. Some have numbers around the outer edge of the watch face, while others have digital numbers. As children we learned how to tell time on the large black and white clock, with an hour hand, minute hand and second hand. Now children have difficulty telling time on this "old fashioned"/ clock, due to the digital age.

Watches are special time pieces, that show one's personality. This piece of jewelry makes a statement to those who see it. Some prefer name brand expensive watches to impress people who see it, while other watches are fun and trendy. Watches have been a special purchase for weddings, graduation, anniversary, birthday, or Christmas gifts. Some of these gifts become family heirlooms, that are passed down from generations to generation. One special heirloom has been grandfathers pocket watch.

The birth of the watch was in the 15th century, for sailors to navigate at sea. Sailors used stars and the local time to determine their route across the sea. If the clock were one minute off, it could deviate their course 28km off their course. So the origin of the watch was out of necessity for a navigation tool.

The German Peter Henlein invented the first portable watch in the 16th century. His watch has a spring mechanism that needed to be wound to keep the proper time. This brand was the Nuremberg eggs. Later Jacob Zech and Gruet, Swiss designers, invented a watch with a resistant spring load that kept the spring tightly wound. This expensive process insured that the clock time stayed accurate. Later the watchmakers used copper which proved to help the watch be even more accurate.

The next design of watchmakers was the wristwatch. Robert Hooke, an Englishman, worked on spring ran balance wheel structure which improved the accuracy in navigation. At the same time a Dutchman, Christiaan Hygens, was working on a similar invention with the balance wheel structure for accuracy.

Wrist watches were not just used in navigation, women began wearing watches in the 19th century. Women's watches were more decorative and trendier, a special jewelry piece. This jewelry was a great gift for husbands to give their wives or girlfriend for anniversaries or birthdays. The First World War had an influence on watchmaking. Soldiers started wearing watches, keeping them on schedule throughout the day in battle. These watches were quartz watches, and ran on batteries, making them cheaper than original watchmakers watches. The original watchmakers became less and less needed for the repairs and designs of watchmaking.

Thousands of watches design and models have been made throughout the years. We have come a long way from the sundial, marked with Roman numerals on the outer edge and Arabic numerals on the inner circle. In ancient times, placing a stick in the ground and placing rocks at North, South, East, and West, making the shadow of the sun tell the time. Wrist watches have certainly made it much easier to tell time throughout our days. Mass production of wrist more exactly on your wrist.

Activities:

- Get a Sudoku Puzzle to work together. Dollar store has them with answers.
- Number Puzzle (next page)

SODOKU PUZZLE

Try to fill in the missing numbers.
The missing numbers are integers between 1 and 6.
The numbers in each row add up to totals to the right.
The numbers in each column add up to the totals along the bottom.
The diagonal lines also add up the totals to the right.

Answer in back of the book

				16
5	6			19
	1	5		13
6		4		18
		2	5	16
22	14	16	14	15

History of the Front Porch

Food:
- Sweet Tea, lemonade, ice cream, popsicle, apple pie, cookies (snicker doodles, ginger snaps, lemon cookies)

Crafts:
- 50 ft. Rope Clothesline (check the Dollar Store), Sharp Scissors, ruler, 6 - 2-inch ring and 6-inch clay pot, for every participant. You can get colored rope.

1) Cut the rope in 8 pieces, 6 feet long.
2) Thread all the ropes into the ring and divide them in half around the ring.
3) Down 4 inches and tie a knot in the rope.
4) Measure down 12 inches and gather 2 strands of the rope and make a knot in them by crossing the rope, right over left and left over right. Do this same knot 2 inches down with the other 3 sets of rope.
5) Go down 3 inches and take one strand from one knot and one from an other knot and tie them together in the same knot pattern. Do this with the other 3 knots.
6) Take a strand from one knot and one from the other knot and tie them together, making a third row of tied knots.
7) Six inches down tie all the strands together in a big knot.
8) Place the clay pot in the rope above the knot. Then you have a plant hanger. Plant hanger is something you might see hanging on a front porch.

History:

One of American's favorite pass time is enjoying a glass of sweet tea on your front porch. When life was easier, people loved relaxing on their front porch, visiting with family and friends, and waving to the passersby.

The evolution of front porches began with the wealthy as a status symbol. The porch began 125 years ago, as a small covering to keep you dry over the front door when it rained. The wealthy would have elaborated, high ceiling, large porches, with decorative finials to show off to the passersby. Porches grew in popularity throughout the years and many looks for a large porch when purchasing a home.

The developing of the larger porch served several purposes throughout the years. The high ceiling helped to keep the sun off the inside rooms of the house, for them to stay cooler in the summer heat. The high ceiling allowed those sitting on the porch to enjoy the summer breeze. The large porch allowed the family to sit on the porch for shade, and to watch the summer rain. The large porch allows the family to leave their windows open without getting the front rooms wet inside.

Greece was the originator of the framed entryway that added a special look to their homes. Porches were called porticos in Greece. British builders brought this look to America and that is why they caught on to the wealthy homeowners.

As the popularity of porches grew, they became larger and some even wrapped around the entire home. These larger porches were called verandas. The large verandas became an extension of the home for parties, reunions, and family gatherings.

What started out as a status symbol for the wealthy, became a item of interest for buyers of homes. Realtor sales of houses with large front porches grew. Families enjoyed using them during all seasons, decorating them for Halloween, Thanksgiving and of course Christmas. Fourth of July you might see them decorated with red, white, and blue swags and flying the American flag.

Porches were not used in the daylight hours, at night families would gather in the cool evening sharing stories of the day or reminiscing about the event of the past. Star gazing was another pass time as you sit at night on your front porch at night. Children's favorite pastime at night was catching lightening bugs and gathering them in a mason jar. Parents watched the giggling children in their porch swing or their rocking chairs. This simpler life allows the parents to relax on the porch and let the worries of the day melt away.

As cities grew and lives became busier and busier, relaxation on a large front porch decreased. Large porches were seen more often in the country where life is a bit slower than in the city. The development of air conditioning further decreased the need for the breeze of a large front porch. Another decline of the front porch sitting was the invention of the television. People replaced interacting in the cool of the evening with sitting in front of the television.

The current generation of home buyers are not as interested in finding a house with a front porch or sitting on a swing watching the neighbors go by. Dan Stalker, a home developer, has brought back homes with front porches, His vision sees the importance of including porches in his newly designed community of houses. His hope is that the trend will return to the carefree days of front porch sitting, and relaxing the cares of the day away, instead of sitting in front of the television or computer for entertainment. Maybe his vision might bring communities back together in his developing neighborhoods.

Activities:
- Discuss with the group what they liked to do on their front porch.
- Write a poem entitled, "Sitting On My Front Porch." You can write it as a group or individually.

Tomb of the Unknown Soldier

Food:
- Clean and cut celery stalks and fill them with cream cheese and pimento cheese to resemble straight soldiers.

Craft:
- Rounded wooden clothespins enough for every participant. Navy, yellow, white, navy acrylic paints. Navy small pompom for hats. Paint brushes (medium and thin brushes) Paint the soldier with a white dress shirt, and navy coat and pants. You need a yellow strip on the sides of the pant legs. Paint a face with sunglasses over the eyes. Finish with a navy pompom hat. These will represent a Soldier who guards the Unknown Soldier tomb.

History:

Located across the Potomac River from Washington, D.C., in Arlington County, Virginia is Arlington National Cemetery. These 624 acres, house 400,000 soldiers who have lost their lives beginning from the Civil War, as well as re-interred dead from earlier wars. These white, uniformed, perfectly aligned, grave markers, are an unbelievable reminder of the thousands of soldiers who lost their lives for our freedom. Located up the hill from this moving sight, is the tomb of the Unknown Soldiers.

The Tomb of the Unknown Soldier is a monument honoring soldiers who have lost their lives in wars but were never identified. A similar memorial can be found in many nations honoring the unidentified soldiers remains. Honoring those who fought for our freedoms, the Tomb of the Unknown Soldier is guarded 24 hour-a-day, 7 days a week, 365 days a year, even at night when the cemetery is closed. There has been a Sentinel Soldier every day, all day since 1937. The shifts are on duty for 24 hour-a-day, with a relief every half hour from April 1st, through September 30th, and every hour from October 1st through March 31st. The relief soldiers are at least four soldiers a shift with some soldiers in training.

The soldiers who stand guard at the Tomb are not deleted from the guard in rain, sleet, snow, or global pandemic. The "Old Guard" as they are called, keep watch as an honor to the fallen soldiers. Our honorable soldiers take meticulous watch over the tomb, even when no one is watching but God. It is an honor to have this job.

The guard team are called Sentinel guards. Once assigned to this guard, these soldiers usually dedicate 18 months of their service to guarding the Tomb of the Unknown Soldiers. Some may serve more or less time if they prefer to make the change. The Sentinel live either in a barracks on Fort. Myer, adjacent to the cemetery, or off base in housing of their choice.

Sentinel soldiers who have the post to guard the Tomb, for at least 9 months, are given the Tomb Guard Identification Badge (TGIB). This wreath pin adorns over 630 soldiers' uniforms, who have guarded the Tomb since its creation in 1958. Prior to this time of the wreath pin, there are hundreds more Sentinel soldiers from 1926 until 1958 who guarded the tomb. Since this post was considered a combat post, women were not allowed to serve in this capacity until 1994. In 1997 that changed with the first female guard, SGT Danyell Wilson, followed by SSG Tonya Bell in 1998, and the third SGT Ruth Hanks in 2015. All who receive this wreath pin, feel a great honor having served this post.

Sentinel guards spend 8 hours making sure their uniform and weapon is perfect for duty. Their uniform is the U.S Army dress blues, sunglasses, and standard military shoes with raised souls. The raised souls have steel tipped toes and "horseshoe" steel plates on the heels. These added features prevent wearing of the souls, smooth movements during the guard, along with the clicking sound marking the 21-gun salute for the deceased. The built-up shoes allow the soldier to stand perpendicular to the ground, without bouncing or bobbing, looking like they are gliding fluidly up and down in front of the Tomb.

The Sentinel guards also wear moist gloves to assist with their grip on their raffle. This allows the movements to be sharp and crisp for rifle inspections. Each guard carries a full functional M14 rifle. Some might not think that this post is not a "real post," but they are considered a combat unit. This rifle comes in handy if an observer tried to charge the Tomb or deface this honored grave.

In the 1920's the Tomb looked much different than it does today. This unguarded grave was flat grassy area that many people used for a picnic site, because of its wonderful view of the city. It was not until 1925 that the 70-ton marble slab, and guards was employed on this site. The next year, a US Army soldier was posted to guard the Tomb during open hours of Arlington Cemetery. In 1927 the guard duty expanded to a 24-hour watch.

Watching the Sentinel guard, the Tomb is an awesome experience. The crowd is silent and the clicking of their taps on their shoes is mesmerizing. Wreaths are placed on the Tomb daily and can be placed there by up to four family members of a Veteran or member of the armed forces. The current President of the United States will be the honored guest, to lay the wreath on the Tomb, on Memorial Day each year. At the end of this moving ceremony, the 24 notes of "Taps," brings a tear to the eyes of those observing this amazing tribute to the fallen unknown soldiers.

Activities:

- Word Search: Tomb of the Unknown Soldiers Puzzle

TOMB OF THE UNKNOWN SOLDIERS PUZZLE

```
U O S L V Z S X T I J B S H V
E J N G F T B E U K U E P Z I
C E M E T E R Y V G N U A O R
S R E I D L O S L O E Q T J G
Q E C Z S X X E N W L X Y I I
B G N A H G X O I H L G Y V N
Q M T T E E T Z A I A Q A C I
A Y O G I G U S Z T F Y R B A
Y C R T N N K W R E A T H R H
V S F I K C E C G I R O N O H
Y F L N I D I L F V F E W F P
Y R O L N M I K Q V G F Y B Q
A W C S D C W N R W U F L I Y
N O B O F M R Y T X N H J E F
A O F B U L H Z Y V X Y V W T
```

ARLINGTON	BUGLE	CEMETERY
CLICKS	FALLEN	GLOVES
HONOR	RIFFLE	SENTINEL
SOLDIER	TAPS	TOMB
UNKNOWN	VIRGINIA	WHITE
WREATH		

History of Baked Alaska

Food:

- Baked Alaska, (see recipe below). Or you can just serve cake, ice cream, and divinity cookies, these items are the three ingredients of Baked Alaska.

Craft:

- A tile for each participant. Dark brown, white, black acrylic paint, and brushes. Use the Alaskan moose pattern to trace with a pencil on the tile. Paint the moose dark brown, with black eyes. Highlighting if desire.

History:

A special dessert, for special occasions, Baked Alaska, is a cake topped with ice cream, and topped in meringue, that has been browned in the oven. It is a delicious dessert. The story of the classic dessert baked Alaska begins far from Alaska, and not with a baker. Instead, it was the American-born physicist and inventor Sir Benjamin Thompson, and Count Rumford whose discovery would lead to the creation of the dessert.

While living in Europe around the turn of the 19th Century, Thompson discovered that the whipped egg whites in meringue made it a very good insulator. By the 1830s, French chefs were using his discovery to create a dish called the "omelet Norwegge," consisting of layers of cake and ice cream covered in meringue, then broiled, writes Maya Silver in a 2016 NPR story entitled "Baked Alaska: A Creation Story Shrouded in Mystery." However, she points out that there are various accounts — Michael Krondl, an associate editor of the Oxford Companion to Sugar and Sweets, says the omelet Norwegge did not appear until the 1890s.

Activity:

Make Baked Alaska. See recipe. **Baked Alaska** - Cake and ice cream dessert topped with meringue -- vary ice cream flavors for your signature dish. I like cherry-burgundy ice cream!

Ingredients (Original recipe yields 16 servings)

2 quarts vanilla ice cream, softened

1 (18.25 ounce) package white cake mix

1 egg

½ teaspoon almond extract

8 egg whites

⅛ teaspoon cream of tartar

⅛ teaspoon salt

1 cup white sugar

Directions

Step 1 Line the bottom and sides of an 8-inch round mixing bowl or deep 8-inch square container with foil. Spread ice cream in container, packing firmly. Cover and freeze 8 hours or until firm.

Step 2 Preheat oven to 350 degrees F (175 degrees C). Grease and flour an 8x8 inch pan.

Step 3 Prepare cake mix with egg and almond extract. Pour into prepared pan.

Step 4 Bake in preheated oven according to package instructions, until center of cake springs back when lightly touched.

Step 5 Beat egg whites with cream of tartar, salt, and sugar until stiff peaks form.

Step 6 Line a baking sheet with parchment or heavy brown paper. Place cake in center. Turn molded ice cream out onto cake. Quickly and prettily spread meringue over cake and ice cream, all the way to paper to seal. Return to freezer 2 hours.

Step 7 Preheat oven to 425 degrees F (220 degrees C).

Step 8 Bake the Alaska on the lowest shelf, 8 to 10 minutes, or until meringue is lightly browned. Serve at once.

DISCOVERING ALASKA PUZZLE

```
N E M W C T J S T A D K P C A
T R A O P Z S E H U O V Z L M
M E E Z O E M L G R G B A G I
A U G H N S T A I O S S D B U
H D S K T D E H L R K D E L S
O M R H Q R W W Y A V J B R P
A A V R E Y O O A S T W A Y N
D P S S G R D N D I X E R A G
L M M L T Y S Z D C B N Y O Q
E G A R O H C N A S E V L O W
Y H U S K Y G D Y H G D U R L
G L A C I E R I Y K S S F J R
L I T X C P F W L N Y A H R E
I L J D Q H R N O O A I X L C
L V V J L O W U P X Q P J K Y
```

ALASKA	ANCHORAGE	AURORAS
BEARS	DARKNESS	DAYLIGHT
DOGS	GLACIER	GOLD
HUSKY	LIGHTS	MOOSE
MUSHERS	NORTHERN	SLED

AUGUST

National Egg Roll Day

Food:

- Egg Rolls, hot mustard sauce, sweet and sour sauce, and assorted teas.
- You could have a Chinese meal along with the egg rolls.

Crafts:

- Get white construction paper, pink and black paint, Q-tips, and rubber bands. Take the black paint and make branches with the black paint. Use the Q-tips and put rubber bands around about 5 Q-tips. Use the Q-tip bundles, and dip them in pink paint and make flower buds up and down the branches. These will be Chinese cherry blossom branches.

History:

When dining at a Chinese Restaurant, many start off their meal, with soup or egg rolls. The egg roll has become a popular food for appetizer, a fun party food, and a midnight snack. The traditional egg roll has been expanded in some restaurants to include other fillers like, mac and cheese, corned beef and cabbage, hamburgers plus their fixings, and Carolina BBQ.

So where did the egg roll begin? Its roots do not go back to China and the egg roll is not that old as a menu item. In 1930, Henry Low, a New York Chef decided to publish a recipe for egg rolls and the craze began. Immigrants and travelers brought the egg roll recipe back from China. Chinese restaurants started selling egg rolls with their eat in and take-out orders. The egg rolls were filled with pork, shrimp, bamboo shoots, scallions, ginger, and garlic, wrapped and fried into a tasty, rolled wrapper.

The newer egg rolls are wrapped with shredded cabbage and carrots, pork, chicken or shrimp, bean sprouts, and seasonings. In 2000's vegetarian versions, and beef filled egg roll options are available. This finger food shows up at parties, weddings and after school snack.

Chinese are not the only connoisseurs of egg rolls. Vietnamese immigrants brought their style of egg rolls to the United States.

Their egg rolls were made with cellophane noodles instead of cabbage. Vietnamese use sweet chili fish sauce, instead of the sweet and sour dipping sauce. They also use a thin rice paper wrap instead of the thicker type wrap for holding the ingredients before frying them in hot grease. Some are still wrapped in the wheat-based thicker wraps and fried in a wok.

Egg rolls are part of the China's New Year's celebrations. It is customary to serve egg rolls to family and friends. February is another time when egg rolls are just the treat to brighten up Valentine's Day dinner. Egg rolls from China to America, has become a favorite for eight decades. If you have not tried an egg roll, you might want to give this favorite treat.

Activities:
- Play Chinese Checkers

Discovering Coffee

Food:
- Coffee Cakes, and different types and flavors of coffee.

Crafts:
- Obtain several glass votive containers from the dollar store. Use tacky glue and glue coffee beans onto the sides. Place a candle inside the glass container when dry. The different flavors of coffee beans can provide a pleasing aroma when the votive is burning.
- Go to a thrift shop and purchase different inexpensive coffee cups. Older cups would provide a fancier look. Paint with glass paint a design onto the sides of the upside-down coffee cups. Purchase a glass votive to put on top. If you have a fancy cup, you can use the saucer to glue on top of the upside-down cup for a more dramatic effect. This will make a decorative display in your kitchen or on your table.

History:

When American's wake up each morning, 64% look forward to beginning the day with a cup of coffee. Coffee drinks date back to between 800 AD and 1500 AD. Goat herders noticed their flocks appear very active after consuming the beans of the coffee plants. A monk noticed the energy exhibited by the goats too and decided to use the coffee beans to make a drink. This monk was looking for something to help him stay up at night decided to try this drink, which was just what he needed to keep him awake at night. This was the first cup of coffee.

Coffee comes from a green cherry fruit which grows along the branches and harvested when ripe. Coffee trees are kept short to allow their growing energy to go towards the fruit of the plant to harvest for coffee. These trees are unusual because they have flowers, green fruit, and ripe fruit on the tree all at the same time. This allows the harvesting of the coffee beans to be a continuous process all year round. But you must be patient to harvest a cup of coffee because after the flower forms on the tree, it takes 5 years for the fruit to ripen. Coffee plants can live 100 years, but their most productive years are between 7 and 20 years of growth. Coffee trees produce

10 pounds of ripen coffee beans, and 2 pounds of green beans per year.

Coffee plants are grown in rich soil, where temperatures are mild, with frequent rain and shaded sun. When looking for a cup of coffee you will find the trees in Hawaii, California, Brazil, Africa, and Vietnam. Brazil is the largest producer of coffee at 30%. Vietnam is the number two at 29% and Ethiopia is third largest at 28%. Vietnam coffee has a strong flavor taste, Africa also has a strong but sweet flavor. Around the world you will find 500 genera of coffee blends and 6,000 species of coffee trees, therefore you will find 25 to 100 blends of coffee tastes from these plants. Other countries where coffee is produced is Mexico, Puerto Rico, Guatemala, Costa Rica, Colombia, Ethiopia, Kenya, Ivory Coast, Yemen, and. Indonesia, every countries coffee blend have different flavors, sweetness, boldness, and strengths once they are processed.

One thing that all the coffee beans have in common is that they start out as green beans and are roasted to bring out the flavors. Each processing of the beans produces the different flavors and tastes. Some other ingredients are added to make the different blends and tastes.

"Coffee" got its name from the Arabic word for wine. The diversions of "coffee" was from the Turkish and Dutch words which was coined in English as "coffee." This rich black liquid is quite the money maker and is the second highest trade commodity next to oils. Four thousand green beans need to be harvested for one pound of coffee. We know if you have purchased a cup of coffee in a specialty shop, you might realize that you will spend $20 per week for your coffee fix. The yearly average that some Americans' spend on coffee is $1,092. The average of 3.2 cups a day are consumed by coffee drinkers each day.

You may have a friend call this black liquid a "cup of Joe." This nick name became popular when Navy Secretary, Josephus Daniels did not want his sailors to be drunk on alcohol, so he outlawed liquor and ordered that coffee be the beverage that was served. Lots of coffee drinkers were born on their ship.

One of the most expensive coffee has a gross production method. This coffee, Kopi Luwak, was developed in Indonesia with the help of an animal called Asian palm civet. These four-legged animals eat the bright red coffee bean cherries until he gets full. He then lies down to partially digest these beans and passes them out as waste. This partial digesting process softens the beans and is supposed to improve the flavor of the coffee. These beans are collected from the civet's droppings and sold for up to $600 per pound. I think I will just enjoy the coffee found in our local grocery stores for my morning pick me up.

Due to the abundance of coffee grown in Brazil, coffee prices are about $1 a pound, the lowest it has been decades. This is good for the consumers, but not for the coffee growers, who make their livelihoods from this product. Next time you order a cup of coffee and it costs more then $1- $2, you might what to think about where you are purchasing this "pick me up" drink.

Those who prefer decaffeinated coffee, so it will not keep you up at night or raise your blood pressure, just know that a trace of caffeine is in decaffeinated coffee too. The caffeine that is removed from the coffee beans is sold to Coca-Cola and processed in their cola drinks. All this talk about coffee has made me want a cup of "Joe," who is with me?

Activities:
- Word search for countries where coffee beans are grown.

COUNTRIES THAT MAKE COFFEE PUZZLE

```
X Y M I C A L Y L A E U I Y A
V Z A G O M I D R T Z N G I Y
E H N R S V D P Y O D L N S H
G P T A T A E M O O V R U X Q
H E E T A G E K N I O I P G T
G P I R R K L E C F H J S N C
Y U V U I M S B I D B T A H K
T H A T C I E L I I C X E V Y
U C B T A Y A X I B R A Z I L
R T V A E C V A I H N W R Y L
K U R M A M W W S C I Q C Q W
E D E B K A A I B M O L O C X
Y N U F H J Q L A Y N E K O S
S C A E V V O D A J A X V L S
P U E R T O R I C O C H U S Q
```

BRAZIL	CALIFORNIA	COLOMBIA
COSTARICA	CUBA	DUTCH
ETHIOPIA	GUATEMALA	HAWAII
INDONESIA	IVORY	KENYA
MEXICO	PUERTORICO	TURKEY
VIETNAM	YEMEN	

National Tooth Fairy Day

Food:

- Mini Marshmallows, they look like teeth.

- Candy Corn. (you can order this if you cannot find it in stores at: candystore.com.

- If no one is allergic to peanut butter, use a recess peanut butter cup and melt mini marshmallows to make a set of teeth.

Crafts:

- Make a tooth fairy pillow for grandchild or to donate to a child. Embroidery something on the fabric,

History:

Parents have spent many hours walking the floor with their babies when they are cutting their teeth Teething rings, numbing medicine and toys with ice inside, are all ways parents try to east their children's pain when they are getting their teeth. Children do not remember much about getting their first tooth, but they do remember losing their first tooth. Northern Europe influenced the United States with the folklore of a mythical characters who flies around looking for teeth under young children's pillows. Somehow when one loses a tooth, the "Tooth Fairy" brings them money that is exchanged for the tooth.

This tradition began with the first tooth but grew to get money for all the teeth lost in childhood. This tradition of the Tooth Fairy was first seen in an article in the Chicago Daily Tribune, in 1908. The author of this idea was Lillian Brown. She thought that a small gift would be a fun tradition for a child who lost a tooth if they placed it under their pillow.

Many think that the Chicago Daily Tribune article was the first Tooth Fairy experiences for children, but research shows this tradition beginning in 1894 in Madrid. Spanish and Hispanic

American cultures shared this Tooth Fairy tradition, exchanging money for the baby teeth.

So how much money should the Tooth Fairy leave under the pillow, or what small gift is appropriate in exchange for baby teeth? I guess it depends on the wealth of the family or the expectations of the child. No matter how much the parent decides to leave from the Tooth Fairy any amount makes the child excited when he awakes in the morning. Another plus for having the Tooth Fairy leave money or a gift is when you have a loose tooth and a reluctant child afraid of having his tooth pulled. The prize can be an incentive to allow his parent to pull the loose tooth.

You hear stories of how some of these teeth are being pulled. My favorite for my son's tooth pulling experience was when he wanted to copy a method used by the Berenstein Bears that we read in a book. The bears put dental floss around the tooth and shut the door. He was excited when he had a loose tooth and wanted to try this method of pulling teeth. Well, you guessed it, we used this method and it worked great. This method offered a distraction, and the tooth was out in a moment. He remembers this fun process to this day and will probably use this method with his child one day too.

So, I must ask, how much money did you get under your pillow from the Tooth Fairy as a child?

Activities:

- Invite a dentist student in to talk about good oral hygiene. Good oral health is important for senior adult health as well as children's health.

History of Girl Scouts and Boy Scouts

Food:
- Make S'mores in the oven. Put half of a graham crackers on a baking sheet. Place a half of a chocolate bar on the graham cracker, and then put a marshmallow on top. Bake at 300 degrees for about 2 minutes.
- Girl Scout Cookies and Boy Scout peanuts and/or popcorn.

Crafts:
1. At a craft store purchase key rings, colored leather shoestrings, and different color beads that will fit on the shoestrings. Cut the shoestring in 10-inch lengths. Fold the shoestring in half and attach it to the ring by taking the tales of the shoestring through the center loop of the shoestring. Next attach the beads in a fun pattern or just use your favorite color. Tie the ends after threading the beads on the shoestring to keep them from falling off. This would be a project that Scouts might make at a meeting or on a camping trip.

2. Make a decoration S'more. You could get small rectangles of thin board the size of a graham cracker and paint them tan. Next cut a smaller piece of rectangular wood for the chocolate, paint it brown. Use 2 circular wood the size of a marshmallow and paint them white. Put each piece on top of each other starting with the graham cracker piece, chocolate piece and then the marshmallow. After it is assembled, put a face on the top marshmallow, and stick arms like a snowman. The marshmallow could be decorated with a hat of any kind.

History:
In 1908 a British man named Baden Powell saw the need for young boys to be engaged in life learning activities. His hope was to help boys progress successfully into manhood. He did not see any one organization created that would raise boys with this goal in mind. So, in 1908, with the joining of many community organizations The Boy Scouts were born. The group did not remain in Britain but became part of Scouting in the United States and rapidly grew to the largest organization in the United States.

The Boy Scouts helped young boys learn life lessons, form friendships, work as a team, and those boys without fathers would have male role models. Scouting helps boys of all ages learn many life skills which would help them be successful. Boy Scouts earn badges on cooking a meal, tying knots, first aid, fitness, leadership, camping, using a compass to navigate, learn about nature, and how to swim, Scouts focus on God and country, so they have a dedicated following

Boy Scout Oath or Promise:

On my honor, I will do my best
To do my duty to God and my country and to obey the Scout Law;
To always help other people;
To keep myself physically strong, mentally awake, and morally straight.

Note that the Boy Scout Oath has traditionally been considered to have three promises.

- Duty to God and country,
- Duty to other people, and
- Duty to self

Boy Scout Law:

A Scout is:

- Trustworthy,
- Loyal,
- Helpful,
- Friendly,
- Courteous,
- Kind,
- Obedient,
- Cheerful,
- Thrifty,
- Brave,

- Clean,
- and Reverent.

Boy Scout Motto: Be Prepared!

Boy Scout Slogan: Do a Good Turn Daily!

The Outdoor Code:

As an American, I will do my best to -

- Be clean in my outdoor manners
- Be careful with fire
- Be considerate in the outdoors, and
- Be conservation minded.

During the Progressive Era in 1912, woman was not allowed to vote. Juliette Gordan, an almost deaf 51-year-old woman from Savannah, Georgia, felt that woman should have the same rights as men did to vote. Wanting to change this double standard she gathered a group of 18 girls and began to teach them courage, confidence, and character in this group of young girls. As this movement grew across America, Juliette's girls became the trail blazers for girls everywhere opening many possibilities for them in life. Out of this group the Girl Scouts were born.

The Girl Scouts was set up for them to earn badges that would give them a variety of experiences from basketball, hiking, swimming, sewing, cooking, astrology and camping to name a few. These experiences sparked a sense of curiosity and a feeling that they could determine their own destiny. Girl Scouts also teaches to help others and working together can be a way to improve the world we live in.

A vision by Juliette Gordon to help girls find their voice in the world, has grown into 2.6 million Girl Scouts, led by 800,000 adults, in 92 countries. Lifelong experiences and friendships have been developed by the group we call Girl Scouts, and together they have made a world of difference in our world.

The Girl Scouts also have an oath or promise:

Girl Scout Promise
On my honor, I will try:
To serve God and my country,
To always help people,
And to live by the Girl Scout Law.

(While saying this, hold up the 3 middle fingers on you left hand)

Girl Scout Law:

I will do my best to be
honest and fair,
friendly and helpful,
considerate and caring,
courageous and strong, and
responsible for what I say and do,
and to respect myself and others,
respect authority,
use resources wisely,
make the world a better place, and
be a sister to every Girl Scout.

Girl Scout Motto: Be Prepared

Girl Scout Slogan: Do a good turn daily.

Whether you are a Girl Scout or Boy Scout, camping is a big part of the program. Learning how to survive in the outdoors while hiking and camping gives Scouts a lot to learn. One of the most fun memory is the campfire roasting hotdogs and S'mores.

As you sit around a campfire with a tray of marshmallows, chocolate bar, graham crackers and an unbent wire coat hanger, your mind might go back to these younger years as a Girl or Boy Scout. Putting a marshmallow on a wire and toasting it over the open flame is the beginning of this delicious treat. While the marshmallow is hot, you smash it between two graham crackers with a half of a chocolate bar for the yummy treat we now call – a S'more. You might want to thank a Girl Scout leader, Loretta Scott Crew, for putting these three ingredients together to form a rich, fun, gooey and delicious treat. In 1927 this "Some More" recipe was published in a Girl Scout publication, Tramping and Trailing with the Girl Scouts.

Girl Scouts are not strangers to treats as every January they sell their ever-popular Girl Scout cookies. The ever-popular Thin Mint, Samosa (Carmel Delights), Tagalongs (Peanut Butter Patties), Do-Si-Dos (Peanut Butter Sandwich), and Shortbread Cookies are some of the first sold by the Girl Scout Troops. The line of cookies has grown to include 9 different choices to choose from. The sales of the cookies help the Troops enjoy outings, camping and supports their meetings. Boy Scouts sell peanuts and popcorn, so your favorite treats all covered.

Girl and Boy Scouts were great steppingstones for young lives to be transformed with lessons they could use throughout life along with, lifelong friendship, and learning to honor God and Country.

Activities:
- Reminisce about who was a Girl Scout or Boy Scout and what experiences they had.
- See if they could remember the Oaths/Promise, Law, Motto, and Slogan
- Do they remember badges they earned?
- Their favorite experiences camping.
- Do they remember any songs they learned in Scouts that they sang around the campfire or while hiking?
- Look up the symbol for Girl Scouts and Boy Scouts and print them off. Pictures of their uniforms and other symbols.

SEPTEMBER

History of the One Room School House

Food:

- Apple pie, apple fritter, apple cake, apples with caramel dip, apple tea and coffee.

Crafts:

- Get small black boards at a craft store enough for every person. Acrylic paint in red, green, brown, and white. Use these paints to make an apple boarder on the frame of the black board. Get white chalk to write your last name on the board or "Welcome" and display it in your kitchen.

History:

If you travel the back country roads enjoying the countryside, you might come across a one-room schoolhouse. The first one room schoolhouse built in 1785, was in Springfield, Vermont. These schools would teach reading, writing, arithmetic, history, and geography, to a class of students 6-year-old to 13 years old. The teachers had to be very creative to be successful at this task.

Most teachers were single women, receiving a low salary for her teaching efforts. The single female teacher lived with one of her student's homes with their family, because single women could not live alone. Another factory for the live-in situation is because teachers paid was very low salaries, making living on their own very difficult.

Originally, one-room schoolhouses development was under the authority of the local church. Churches hoped to help students learn to read so that they would read the Bible and receive the religious training. Having the churches lead education was not a problem then, because the community had the same religious beliefs. Around the 1800's when England no longer ruled, the shift to governmental run schools began. In the 1830's School Districts were developed to run schools and tuition for attending school was initiated.

Schools were much different in the early days of education. The school days lasted from 9 a.m. to 4 p.m. with 2 recesses of 15 minutes each, and one hour given for lunch. Many of the lessons were memorizing the information and reciting it back to the teacher. The class size could be up to 30 students per class. Students were also responsible for the maintenance of the building. Older children would take care of gathering and cutting wood and cleaning out the fireplace. Younger children assignment was to clean the chalkboards, erasers, and sweeping the floors.

Schoolhouses were not equipped with pluming, so water had to be carried in for drinking and washing your hands and bathrooms were outhouses. Not many modern conveniences were available, but at least the children were warm in the winter months due to the fireplace.

Today, one-room schoolhouses still exist. The numbers have dwindled over the last 100 years from 190,000 schools to 400 still in operation today. Thirty-three states still have operating one-room schoolhouses across America. These schools can be in Alaska, Delaware, Missouri, New York, and Pennsylvania.

In the 1920's the use of school buses made it possible for children to be picked up over miles and carried to school for educational purposes. Large government run schools began to replace the one-room schoolhouses. Most of the one-room schoolhouses replacements with the larger community schools by the end of World War II. You can still find one-room schoolhouses in Alaska and Australia.

We can all thank Roberto Nevelis, from Venice, Italy, for the idea of having additional work to do once your school day was completed. In 1095, he introduced the idea of working on projects and homework that needed to return with you the next day of school. Thanks to Roberto, our after-school play time was cut short due to more schoolwork at home.

Activities:
- Have a spelling bee with the participants
- Have math problems to complete
- Word search about school

ONE ROOM SCHOOLHOUSE PUZZLE

```
B G N I T I C E R M G S S H C
A L G K I S W B E D R S C C U
S J A M L D I M S E Y O I N R
I T V C I A O L H I A T E U H
V P N Y K R H C I L R L N L U
W R H E I B A C A W I L C I C
R R D Z D E O C B C T A E R Z
K C I O T U H A R X H B E R R
O N P T X L T G R O M C V G G
G O D R I C Y S N D E F Q H S
R E A D I N G Z M S T G I M H
J A C K S R G U S V I U E F C
E L P P A D M V L N C O T D R
V F Y R M J H M Z L P P F A F
T T S Y H Q B E T S G J C H G
```

APPLE	ARITHMETIC	BALL TOSS
BLACK BOARD	CHALK	JACKS
LUNCH	MEMORIZING	POEMS
READING	RECESS	RECITING
SCIENCE	STUDENTS	TAG
TEACHER	WRITING	

National Chocolate Pretzel Day

Food: Chocolate covered pretzels. Use dark, milk and white chocolate. Serve coffee, tea, or water.

Crafts:
Use 16 small twisty pretzels, 1 ½ yard of ribbon. Lace the ribbon through the pretzel. Stagger the 8 pretzels on top of the bottom pretzels. Lace them in a circle and tie a bow on the top. You can use them to hang in the trees for birds to enjoy for the fall/winter months. See photo of wreath.

History:
October 7 is Chocolate Covered Pretzel Day. This yummy treat enjoyed whether dipped in dark chocolate, milk chocolate, or white chocolate for a delicious treat. How did the chocolate pretzel get started? A German baker, Julius Sturgis opened a community bakery in his Pennsylvania home, in the 1500 where he made and sold pretzels. Sturgis had an idea to put chocolate and pretzels together, but in those days', chocolates was a drink. In the late 1800's a process for making chocolate harden was developed. The process separated solid chocolate from the butter, that made it runny, and then it could harden to make other items.

Separating the chocolate from the butter, gave bakers and candy makers a completely new creation. The chocolate used to make a variety of chocolate candies and another solid sweet salty treat was born. Casparus van Houten Sr was -the brain of covering the pretzel with chocolate, making a sweet-salty tasting treat.

Pretzel rods, twists, knots, and rings, dipped in chocolate and decorated with brightly colored sprinkles, nuts, and cookie crumbles. If you like sweet and salty taste together, this treat will be the perfect choice for snickers.

Chocolate covered pretzels would not be around without first having the pretzel. The origin of the pretzel began with the Catholic Church. Pretzels were the perfect food when meat, dairy and eggs were prohibited during lent. The easily unleavened bread dough came over to America on the Mayflower with the Pilgrims. These soft pretzels enjoyed alone in the early years, but today we add cheese dip, cinnamon and icing, or mustard. As the pretzels took on different shapes and sizes, and they cooked them to a crispy harder treat, the idea for chocolate dipping began.

Chocolate dipped pretzels is a nice treat. Homemade versions made for holiday gifts for family and friends. Two sisters in Brooklyn, NY have a gourmet pretzel store, Fatty Sundays, inspired by their mother. Their specialty treats use high quality chocolates, toffee, birthday cake, and salted caramel when they dip their pretzel treats. The two sisters sell specialty pretzels gift-boxed all year round.

Activity:

Make chocolate dipped pretzel rods. Use sprinkles, nuts, or cookie crumbs to decorate the chocolate while warm.

History of Bowling

Food:
- French fries, burgers, hot dogs, popcorn, and sodas, as bowling alley food.

Crafts:
- Give each participant a Pringle can decorate with faces to use as bowling pins.
- Call bowling alleys to see if they have some discarded pins that you could decorate as a scarecrow, or snowman. For the scarecrow, use burlap to glue onto the top of the pin for a hat. Underneath the edges of the hat, around the eyes use raffia for hair. Paint on eyes or use google eyes. Tie a piece of cloth on the bottom. Or you can use the pin and paint it white for a snowman. Paint eyes on the skinny top, or use google eyes. Tie a piece of fabric around the neck. Put buttons down the front, and a piece of orange paper, foam, or pipe cleaner for the nose.

History:
Around 5,000 BC in Ancient Egypt was the earliest form of the game of bowling. The game was played with rough stones, or objects that the Egyptians would set up and roll another stone towards to know them down for points. As time went on, this game changed from tall rocks to a variety of other objects until it finally became a tall candle shaped "pin" that was used for the game.

Bowling was played with a variety of traditions from ten-pin bowling, to nine-pin bowling, candle pin bowling, duck pin bowling and five-pin bowling. Some even took this game outside in the lawn and called it lawn bowling and bocce; many of the different styles of bowling are still enjoyed today.

The rules are still the same today. If you get all the pins down in one ball, it is known as a "strike." If you need two balls to get a lot of pins down, it is called a "spare." If you roll the ball and end up with pins on both sides of the lane, is called a "split." When recording a "strike" or "split," you record and additional 10 along with whatever pins you get down on your next turn. If it is a "strike," you get two ball totals, and a "spare," you get one ball total added to your score.

The ten-pin and candle bowling, the player uses a smaller ball about the size of a soft ball. The weight on this ball is also about 3 ½ lbs. When playing ten-pin the balls are a lot larger, about a basketball size and range from 8 lbs. to 16 lbs. The larger ball also has three holes drilled in the ball in a triangle formation for your thumb and two fingers to hold onto the ball while you swing it beside you and then forward to release it at the pins.

Bowling came to New York City in 1895, and the leagues caught on quickly. The sport of bowling was something that many people could do, with little or athletic ability. Oh, course as you play and practice, your skill level will improve. The sport of bowling is something you can do by yourself, or as a team. I have heard some say they like this sport because the ball comes back to you, unlike golfing. Bowling is also an affordable sport, especially when you play in a league.

League bowling also brings friends and acquaintances together for an evening of fun and exercise. In 1840's the game of ninepin was popular with gamblers, but later banned in some states. I guess fun competitions of gambling when bowling continues with many today.

Bowling is a fun pastime sport, but if you hear someone call you a "turkey," that is a good thing. That means you just got your third "strike" in a row which gives you lots of points. If you continue to get all "strikes for 10 frames, you will have a perfect score of 300 and receive a patch for your bowling shirt at the end of the season. The average bowler bowls between 130-150, but beginner bowlers get on average of 78 pins down in a game.

Activities:
- Bowling game on the Wii video system
- Purchase a bowling set and bowl games. Make teams, team names, and keep score for 5-10 frames. Give out small awards for the winning team. These can be purchased at a party store.
- Short on funds, save empty liter bottles and use them for bowling pins. Get a small softball or rubber kick ball to bowl with.
- Use empty Pringles containers as bowling pins.

National Juke Box Day

Food:
- Burgers, milkshakes, cokes, fries, whip cream and cherries.

Crafts:
- To make a black and white place mat. Get black and white construction paper, enough for each participant. Fold the black piece in half, placing the shorter sides together. On the fold, cut slits every inch, cutting it to one inch from the other edge. Then with the white paper, cut into one-inch strips from shorter side. Take the white pieces and weave it up and down until you reach the other side. The next row starts opposite then your last strip. When you finish, you will have a black and white checkerboard place mat, like most soda shop floors.

History:

Students could not wait to get out of school for the day, head to the soda shop to get a coke, burger, fries and pop a nickel into the Jukebox. This automated music box held all your favorite songs of the time, and some oldies. As you made your music selections, you would watch the electronic arm scroll through the records and choose the one you had picked. Diners today have this iconic Jukebox of the past playing our old 50's and 60's music for 5 songs for 25 cents.

The Jukebox introduced to the United States in 1940, invented by Louis Glass's nickel-in-the-slot phonograph. Glass invented the jukebox in 1889 to bring music to the Palais Royale Saloon in San Francisco. His music-making machine was a modified Edison's phonograph, run by battery. Many bars and saloons had a Jukebox in the corner for the patrons to enjoy.

When the sitcom "Happy Days" began, the students would hang out at the local soda shop, "Arnolds," were the jukebox provided the right song for the different situations. "The Fonz" often wanted to dance with one of the beautiful girls hanging around him, so he would go to the Jukebox and bang on the machine for the song. It was always interesting to see what song would play.

The first Jukebox cost 15 cents to play raising $4,000 in six months. Today to hear music from the Jukebox is $1 to hear five songs.   In 1998, Digital Jukeboxes came on the scene.   Introducing Digital Jukeboxes designed to keep track of the songs played. Keeping track is important because bars have to pay royalties on the songs played. Customers paying to listen to favorite songs is costly for the owners but paying for the song offsets the royalties owed the artists.   The digital jukeboxes save the bar owner $7,000-$15,000 in licensing fees.

Some Diners still have the old jukeboxes at the table or in the restaurant where patrons can drop in some coins and take a walk back to the simpler days.   As your favorite songs play, you can reminisce snuggling in a booth with your boyfriend or girlfriend, while you share an ice cream soda.   Fond memories come flooding back of the past.   So, if you want to take a walk down memory lane, you might want to head to a local diner to play the Jukebox.

Activities:

- Write a poem about going to the soda shop.   You can write a Haiku style poem, first line is 5 syllables, second line 7 syllables, third line 5 lines.

Example of Haiku Poem style:

An Ocean Voyage
As Waves Break Over the Bow
The Sea Welcomes Me

History of the Eiffel Tower

Food:
- Quiche, macaroons, and eclairs. To drink offer coffee and tea.

Crafts:
- Use clay to build a model of the Eiffel Tower.
- Clip Art outline of the Eiffel Tower. Use straws cut to different sizes to glue onto the paper to make an Eiffel Tower. If participants have agile fingers, use yarn or string to fill in the Eiffel Tower,

History:

When you think of France, your thoughts immediately go to their famous landmark, the Eiffel Tower. Over 200 million visitors have visited this famous structure.

To celebrate the French Revolution, the French government held a competition contest for the best designing of an "iron tower." In 1889, the government held a Universal exhibition of the iron tower structures. Gustav Eiffel was the winner out of the 107 entries. The engineer and entrepreneur, Gustav Eiffel, worked with Stephen Sauvestre, architect, and two engineers Maurice Koechlin and Emile Nouguier to construct this famous tower.

The Eiffel Tower was a unique 300 meters tall building. This manufactured structure built from wrought iron latticework arches and trusses. Although the structure is 986 feet tall, and weighs 7,300 tons, constructed in a light and airy design. The construction took 18,038 pieces and over two million rivets. The unique lace looking statue has attracted visitors from all over the world each year. January 26, 1887 was the year they broke ground on this wonderful structure.

The original tower did not have an elevator, but five hydraulic elevators installed in June of 1889. This great addition allowed visitors to stop at different observation platforms along the ride up to the top. Part of the curve look of the Eiffel Tower is due to the paint job of the tower, and painting takes place often to keep the design.

During the construction of the Eiffel Tower, many thought it was an eyesore and did not like the construction of the building. Now days, engineers and architects' schools study the design of the construction and incorporate the design in new creations.

The ribbon cutting for the Eiffel Tower was Eiffel himself, climbing to the top of the tower and raising the French flag on the top of the tower. On March 31, 1889, the Eiffel Tower was the tallest building, until 1929, when the Chrysler building completed in New York.

The Eiffel Tower was supposed to be a temporary structure lasting only twelve years, but it became such a popular tourist attraction they it was not torn down. This structure has lasted over a century and houses the broadcasting antenna on top. Since it has become the structure everyone thinks of when you mention France, it is highly unlikely that this building will not remain as an icon in France for another century.

Activities:
- Write the first letter of **E I F F E L   T O W E R** across the top of a white board.   Or use the sheet below to work individually.

On the side of white board write:
- Names beginning with each of the letters in the word.
- States that begin with each letter.
- Food that begins with each letter.
- Something in the room that begins with each letter.
- Peoples names that begin with each letter.
- Clothing item that begins with each letter.

DESCRIBING THE EIFFEL TOWER

E

I

F

F

E

L

T

O

W

E

R

OCTOBER

History of the Swiss Army Knife

Food:

- Protein bars, nuts, dried fruits, veggie chips, coffee, tea. Items you might use on a camping trip, hike or carry in the military.

Craft:

- Make a dragonfly using 2 plastic knives and one plastic spoons. Using the backside of the spoon circle as a head, and the 2 knives as wings. With back side of the spoon facing up, glue two plastic knives crossed half way up the spoon handle. When the glue dries, paint the dragonfly with blue and green paint. Glue small google eyes on the dragonfly head. You could pick up real silverware from a consignment shop or Goodwill, to use to make these dragonflies.
- Use plastic knives to paint a picture. You can use the cutting edge and the flat edge to make different designs and techniques. You could also use other plastic silverware to paint with. Many designs can be made with the different plastic silverware.
- Collect silverware from Goodwill or consignment shop and make a wind chime. You will need 1/4 inch dowel rods, cut in 6 inch sections to use as a cross bar to hand the silverware onto, and thin neutral color twine. Attach the silverware onto twine of various lengths onto the crossed dowel rods. The dowel rods can be glued in a cross or tied with twine in the center piece.

History:

As you see someone who needs a bottle opened, a screw tightened, a nail filed or something cut, you might see them reach into their pocket and pull out a Swiss Army. Many people, especially men, carry a Swiss Army knife with them every day. Tourist visiting Switzerland, look for Swiss Army knives to take home as souvenirs for their male friends. Those who want to be ready for anything, carry this handy tool with them wherever they go. At home or around the world these knives come in handy. They have been used in city adventures, fishing, underwater adventures, mountain trails, and some even have observed their use in outer space.

The Swiss Army knife company was founded in 1884, by Karl Elsener, in Ibach, Switzerland. He and his colleagues produced the first knives used in the Swiss Army. A year later, most of his colleagues left the company to pursue manufacturing a lower cost Swiss Army knife. Being a man of principles and pride, Elsenser continued making the knife according to his process in order to make what he felt was a more substantial tool.

His competition with Wester, the other knive company, made Elsenser incur substantial loss in his company.

Elsenser's company was solicited to produce the 15,000 knives needed to supply the Swiss Army, but due to his financial difficulties, he had to join with a German Company, 300 miles across Swiss boarders for assistance with this order. Because Elsenser teaming up on this project, there became two Swiss Army knife companies, Elsenser's and Westers & Company, the German company. Elsenser's patent in 1897, allowed him to be known as the "Original Swiss Army Knife Company," and Wester's to be known as the "Genuine Swiss Army Knife Company." On the death of Elsenser's mother, in 1909, Elsenser changed the name to "Victoria" in honor of his mother. Later, in 1921 the company name was renamed to "Victorinox." The "inox" part of Victorinox is the French abbreviation for stainless steel This additional abbreviation added to Victoria allowed consumers the company making the knife as well as what it was made of incorporated within their name.

Since the late 1880's, Swiss Army knives have been part of the uniform for the Swiss Army men and women. In the field this knife could assist soldiers to open a can of food, or to fix or disassemble their rifle with only one multi-purpose knife. These knives can also be used to get free from or get through heavy brush or twine. It is a very helpful portable tool out in the field at war.

Victorinox started making surgical equipment to expand his knife company, as well as Swiss cutlery. As the production grew, Elsener decided to expand on the Swiss Army knife design having more tools incorporated within the knife handle. In 1896 the spring handle design allowed for many tools to be held on both sides of the handle. This new design featured a small second cutting blade, corkscrew and wood fiber grip handle. The new design also had an iconic cross and shield so their knives could be easily identified.

Today, Swiss Army knives are available in 100 different models, highlighted in their showroom in Ibach, Switzerland. Victorinox manufactures over 45,000 of these pocket knives each day with 34,000 going out of the store each day to customers. These sales reach to over 100 countries around the world, giving Switzerland a good ambassador for Victorinox.

Victorinox has expanded their products including, kitchen knives, watches, luggage and fragrances to name a few. Although the German company Westers & Co. was only 300 miles from the Swiss boarder, the actual first Swiss Army knives were manufactured in Germany in 1891. This iconic knife, which can be found in a variety of styles, is used and enjoyed by hunters, fishermen, military personnel, and consumers of all types around the world.

Activities:
- Discuss how you are your spouse used the knives throughout the day.
- How did you use this knife in your Military Service.

National Pumpkin Day

Food:

- Pumpkin pie, pumpkin roll, and/or pumpkin muffins and pumpkin coffee.

Crafts:

- Carve pumpkins with each participant, or paint faces on the pumpkins.
- Use craft pumpkins and get push pins with decorative tops to make a design on the pumpkin. This decorative pumpkin can be used as a centerpiece for your Fall table.
- You can also use the pumpkin indentations and draw black lines down each one. Next draw scallops from one line to the next making a spider web. Purchase fake spiders and put a few around the pumpkin. It makes a great Halloween decoration.

History:

As the summertime ends and Fall is in the air, many people are looking forward to pumpkin foods and drinks. Pumpkins not only make tasty treats to usher in the Fall, but they also add a beautiful pop of color with a variety of color and sizes of pumpkins. Other fun Fall activities families look forward to are visiting the pumpkin patch for corn the maze, apple picking, cider, hayrides and of course choosing the perfect pumpkins to carve and decorate with for Halloween and Thanksgiving.

By October 26th, the pumpkin craze is in full swing, and folks are looking forward to their favorite holiday pumpkin pie. The oldest mention of pumpkin seeds, dates to the 7000 and 5500 BC from Mexico. The word was formed from the Greek word "pepon" which means large melon.

Most recently pumpkins were bred to not only be orange, but they developed to produce white, yellow, and green pumpkins. White pumpkins add a elegant twist to the original orange pumpkins. Many couples planning to marry in the Fall, use the white pumpkins to decorate at their Fall weddings. The United States produces 1.5 billion pounds of pumpkins, with 45 different varieties. The top state for pumpkin production is the state of Illinois.

Pumpkins are hardy produce, growing on every continent except Antarctica. Surprisingly, the largest pumpkin recorded was grown in Wisconsin topping out at 1,810 pounds and was as large as a trash dumpster. To help the growth of his pumpkin, the farmer used seaweed, cow manure, and fish emulsion to help the growth of his pumpkin.

When families go to their pumpkin patch searching for the right pumpkin, they cannot wait to get home to carve their face into the flesh. This job begins with cutting off the top, and digging out the "guts," made up of pumpkin seeds and the slimy pulp before they can create the face on their pumpkin.

National Pumpkin Day is a nonofficial holiday celebrated on October 26 celebrating and giving thanks for the development of the pumpkin. Cultivators spent lots of time and energy perfecting the pumpkin, and then developing different pumpkin colors. After Halloween fall festivals might include a "Pumpkin Chucking" device to send your carved pumpkin flying. Some festivals had pumpkin chucking contests made up of teams who have built a variety of catapults. Just an added Pumpkin season fun events to look forward to each Fall.

So slice yourself a piece of pumpkin pie, and add lots of whipped cream, and enjoy celebrating National Pumpkin day with your favorite friends. while remembering what you are thankful for.

Activities:

- Use the word - **T H A N K F U L** and think of things that you are thankful for that begins with each letter. This can be done as a group or individually.

WHAT WE ARE THANKFUL FOR

T

H

A

N

K

F

U

L

N

E

S

S

National Fire Pup Day

Food:
- Chili, with saltine crackers and a variety of hot sauces. This might be a food served at a Fire House
- Black beans and rice.

Quick Black Beans and Rice

Black beans and rice are the most nutritious and well-balanced meal in the world! Try adding your favorite chutney or salsa to this dish when you serve it!

prep: 5 mins   cook: rice with the instructions of the package

Black Beans:

Ingredients

1 tablespoon vegetable oil

1 onion, chopped

1 (15 ounce) can black beans, undrained

1 teaspoon dried oregano

1 (14.5 oz.) can stewed tomatoes

½ teaspoon garlic powder

1 ½ cups uncooked instant brown rice

Directions In large saucepan, heat oil over medium-high. Add onion, cook and stir until tender. Add beans, tomatoes, oregano and garlic powder. Bring to a boil; stir in rice. Cover; reduce heat and simmer 5 minutes. Remove from heat; let stand 5 minutes before serving.

- Chocolate cupcakes with white icing and black polka dots. White cupcakes with chocolate icing with white polka dots.

Crafts:
- Dalmatian dog planter. Use a 4 - 6-inch clay pot. Paint the pot white with black spots. Use google eyes for the eyes and paint a black triangle nose and black mouth. Uses black foam

for long dog ears. Plant an herb in the pot when finished to
have herbs to use over the winter cooking.

History:

When you think of the mascot for the local Fire Department,
your mind immediately goes to the black and white spotted dog, the
Dalmatian. This cute dog became part of the Fireman Squad in the
1700s. Dalmatians were trained as carrier dogs for rescuing people
from firers.

Fires were originally put out by horse drawn water trucks. These
water wagons would show up to the fire and put out the fire. The
Dalmatian was drawn to horses, so you would always find them
running alongside the horse drawn water wagons to the local fire.
This energetic dog breed soon became the Fire Departments mascot.

Before long, Dalmatian puppies traveled around to schools and
civic centers to educate children and the community about fire safety.
The black and white Dalmatian puppies drew the children in, allowed
them to learn about fire safety.

The New York City Fire Department is one Fire House that was
credited for using and training fire dogs. It was during that time; the
Westminster Dog Show observed the skills of the carrier Dalmatians
and saw a new category for their dog show competition. The first
year in the competition, the Dalmatian named "Mike" from New
York Engine Company 8, won the show. Their tradition of including
the Firefighter Dalmatians dogs, became part of the Westminster
Dog Show for the next 30 years.

In 1905 an article was written about how the Fire Fighter's
Dalmatian's mascot has kept this breed popularity alive. Although
Dalmatian's are not needed in the same way in fire rescues, they have
become part of the Firefighter's family spreading smiles about the
fire house.

FIREFIGHTER WORD JUMBLE

GITRREEFFIH

SOHE

MTOAANDLAI

XEA

OTOSB

GONEYX

KASM

DDRLEA

National Left-handed Day

Food:

- Pineapple upside-down cake (cake that is opposite from most other cakes), Coffee and tea.

Craft:

- Hand print cut-out bat. Trace your right and left hand on black construction paper. Put the palms of each cut-out hands together with glue. Use google eyes and put on the center for eyes of your bat. Use bats and ghosts as Halloween decorations.

- Hand print cut-out Ghost. Trace your hands on white paper. Glue google eyes on the palm part of the hand print with the fingers hanging down.

History:

Ten percent of people across the world have one thing in common – they are left-handed. This means 700 million left-handers are around the globe, must put up with a right-handed world. It is not easy being left-handed, because everything from scissors, spiral notebooks, desks and doorknobs, designs are for right-handed people. As time goes on, manufacturers are more sensitive to the left-handed users of everyday items.

Throughout history, many looked at left-handed people as possessed by the devil, unclean spirits, or even witches. Some feel that the devil himself is left-handed. As people realize that being left-handed is due to a genetic link, society has changed their minds about left-handed people and have adjusted everyday items for those who are left-handed.

Scientists feel that a single gene, determines whether someone is right-handed or left. Ten percent of the population has the left-handed traits. Oxford University has discovered that the genes in handedness and twins are similar and controls the different sides of the brain. Twenty one percent of twins are left-handed. The study showed that left-handed people have superior verbal skills.

Science shows that the right side of the brain controls the left side of the body and vice versa. Our bodies have the right side of the brain controlling the motor behavior, and the left side of our brain controls the fine motor skills like writing. These differences might be the differences we see in individuals.

Right-handed people, for the most part, have set up our world. So left-handed people have become ambidextrous. They have learned to use right-handed scissors and use right-handed desks. This group can adapt, which might be a positive skill in life.

Hand dominance does not follow set rules. For example, if both parents are right-handed, there is a 1 in 10 chance of having a left-handed child. If both parents are left-handed, the child has a 4 in 10 chance of being left-handed.

Why do left-handed writers have a poor reputation for neat writing? Left-handed people face a lot of difficulties in everyday life. Handwriting can be particularly hard for lefties, especially if they are taught by a right-handed person, as the grip of the pen and formation of letters is different.

Activities:

● Have the right-handed participants' write their name, today's date, birthday, favorite food, and birthplace with their non-dominant hand.

Friday the Thirteenth

Food: Black cat cupcakes (food and craft) look for directions on internet, Yo-yo cookies and black tea, black coffee, or cola.

Crafts: Use clay and mold a cat, or bake black cat cupcakes

History

When the calendar has a Friday in the month that is the 13th, many people want to stay home in bed. Remaining in bed would eliminate the fear of bad luck due to a variety of possible superstitions happening throughout their day. They would cross their fingers or toes hoping not to spy a black cat cross in their path, or drop a mirror breaking it into pieces, both are to bring about bad luck, the latter for 7 years. Watch out for the full moons – surely chaos will ensue.

Most people have participated in a superstition during their life. If you have read your horoscope, walk down the street, and not step on a crack, avoid a black cat walking in your path, knock on wood for luck, or read a fortune from a fortune cookie, you have participated in a form of superstitions. Another form of superstition is wearing the same socks for your ball game, doing the same routine, or eating the same meals – all three to bring you luck for the game.

The word superstition first shows up in English in the 15th century. A superstition is a practice or irrational belief that makes individuals act or responds to a natural event.

Webster's Dictionary defines superstition as:

a: belief or practice resulting from ignorance, fear of the unknown, trust in magic or chance, or a false conception of causation

b: an irrational abject attitude of mind toward the supernatural, nature, or God resulting from superstition.

c: a notion maintained despite evidence to the contrary

The best way to learn about superstitions is to read some of them from around the world.

Fun Superstitions from other countries

In Russia celebrating or saying Happy Birthday before one's birthday arrived would give them bad luck. In Mexico if you have mirrors hanging across from one another, like you might see in a dressing room, invites the devil into your home.

The Japanese have several superstitions that deal with chopsticks. They say if you put your chopsticks down in your food it resembles the incense used at a funeral or resembles a number 4 which is an unlucky number in Japan. Also, never point your chopstick at anyone, for that is considered to be rude. If you give a gift that is sharp, such as a knife, you need to include a coin so as not to sever your friendship.

In the Philippines, it is tradition following a funeral that people do not return home immediately as you might take the bad spirits home. Usually, they would go to a restaurant instead. This superstition was called "papa."

Lithuania does not believe in whistling while you work, at least not inside. They believe it invites evil in your house.

If you want to make a toast in Germany, you want to make sure you have anything in your glass but water. To toast with water is to wish those you are with to death. You might want to choose wine or beer depending which side of the country you are in.

In Japan, avoid sleeping with your head facing North because that was how they buried they dead, so the living had to face some other direction while sleeping. But if you are in Africa you might find the heads of the beds facing West for good luck.

In Britain, the superstition is to refrain from placing shoes on the table, as that is how they indicate someone has died. Clearly, it is bad luck.

In America, if your left hand itches, money is coming to you, but if the right hand itches, you are going to lose money. In Turkey it was the opposite hands, right get money while left lose money.

Do not play with a pair of scissors in Egypt. This idle activity will bring you bad luck.

The French consider stepping in dog poop to be a lucky event. Along those lines, in Russia if you are pooped on by a bird it supposed to bring you wealth.

Owls are unlucky in man nations. In Egypt they are a sign that bad news is coming. In Italy, an owl getting in your house is a sign of a death in your family.

If you do not like winter, keep your knitting in the house. Knitting outside in Iceland prolongs winter, which would not be something they would want to prolong with their frigid weather.

In 1933 yo-yo's were banned in Syria due to their use would cause a drought.

You need to plan your haircuts in India, so they will not fall on Tuesdays. Haircuts on Tuesday can cause you bad luck.

Yellow flowers in Russia would not be a good gift. This bouquet would mean you are cursing the receiver with infidelity. Who would think spilling water behind someone by accident is good luck in Serbia? Are you wondering why bells were used at weddings? In Ireland bells on wedding your wedding dress are used to ward off evil spirits. Brides did not want these evil spirits to ruin their wedding.

If you do not like goat meat, there is a good reason not to eat it in Rwanda. Women thought it would cause facial hair to grow. In Canada, if a pregnant woman ignores her food cravings, she will deliver a fish head child according to superstition.

In Canada, if a pregnant woman ignores her cravings, she will deliver a fish head child. In Korea have pregnancy superstitions. Women cannot eat asymmetrical foods because this will cause you to deliver an ugly baby.

Walking backwards in Portugal will show the devil which way you are going. So, stay on the straight and narrow path and keep moving forward. Talking to a friend and saying the same word at the same time will cause you not to get married. To stop this bad luck, you must put your finger on your nose. Singing for your supper is not allowed in the Netherlands, unless you want to sing to the devil for food. Watch out for the rain in the Philippines, especially if you are wearing red. Superstition has it that you will attract lightening.

If you do not have a date for New Year's Eve in Spain, just take a bunch of grapes. Eating 12 grapes at midnight to have good luck for the year. Some see a cemetery and hold their breath, but in Japan they hide their thumbs to save their parents lives.

When on a date or in a group and an awkward silence occurs, many feels that angels are passing over head. What a wonderful thought. In Sweden everyone looks out for manholes instead of sidewalk cracks. If you accidentally step on a manhole with an "A" on it, you will have a broken heart and bad luck.

Japanese do not have nail salons open after the sun goes down due to the belief that cutting your nail after the sun goes down would cause a premature death.

Another after sunset superstitions is in Turkey. Chewing gum after dark is believed to chewing on dead flesh. Another Turkish superstition in not to jump over a child it will make them short. A British tradition is to carry an acorn to stay young forever.

In Brazil, do not let your purse touch or be on the floor. It is bad luck financially.

Activities: List or discuss the common superstitions you have heard over the years.

Word find activity:

SUPERSTITION PUZZLE

```
U R W B U T A C K C A L B D R
E T R W E P V S I S K J J E K
B R O K E N M I R R O R D L N
S W C H Y K O H J L Z D L F O
V T W A L C J B S O A E I Y C
U C E U T A I M H L P N P U K
Y D M P Z L D D R S D V B Y O
A K T U O B E E M A I K K R N
X M J S P N D I P G V W C K W
R V M K G N C E M P B T Z H O
S T F E U R N R I N M I B R O
D U H K D N I U A U I Y R I D
N N L U Y S R N X C E Q M J W
U A Y V L K A T I Z K V Z V D
W S A L T T O O F T I B B A R
```

BLACK CAT

BROKEN MIRROR

SALT

FIND A PENNY

KNOCK ON WOOD

RABBITFOOT

WALK UNDER LADDER

SPELL

STEP ON CRACK

WISHBONE

188

Information on the Fall Equinox and Summer Solstice

Food:

- You could serve round foods to represent the earth. Some ideas would be cookies, pizzas, biscuits with jelly, bagels.

Crafts:

- Use leaf patterns. (See below). Take a piece of wax paper for each participant. Trace around the leaves with black marker. Use small pieces of tissue paper and glue them onto the wax paper. After the glue dries, cut out the leaves and use them to decorate the windows.

- Use leaf patterns and trace them onto a sheet of white construction paper, or watercolor paper. Take shaving cream and put on a cookie sheet, enough to dip the paper into the shaving cream so that it covers the paper. Use different color food color and drip color into the shaving cream. You may want to use red, green, yellow, and orange so they are the leaves will be the correct colors of nature. After you drop color into the shaving cream, take a straw or toothpick and mix the colors around. When you like the design, turn the backside of the paper into the shaving cream and push down gently. Then you will need to take a squeegee to remove the excess shaving cream. When it dries, cut out the leaves. You could hang them on string to hang around the room or tape to the windows.

History:

The definition of the word "Equinox," comes from the Latin words equal and night. It is when the daytime and nighttime hours are nearly equal in hours during the 24-hour day. The Earth orbits around the sun at a certain angle. Half of the year, the tilt is towards the sun in the Northern Hemisphere. During this time, the daylight hours are longer and sunnier. As the Earth rotates around the sun, the tilt changes making less hours of sun and more hours of darkness. The two times of year are Summer Solstice and Winter

Solstices.   Daylight becomes shorter and the days head towards cooler weather. This tilt of the Earth is in the Southern Hemisphere.

Summer Solstice is peaks about June 20, and winter Solstice peaks December 21. During these times, the sun's pathway is the furthest from the Equator, the extreme weather differences. An interesting fact about these two days of the year is the sunrise is due east and sets exactly due west.

Equinox and Solstice studies to determine prehistoric details has been Archaeologists studies for many years. Some of the studies took place in the UK at Stonehenge and New Grange, while others were discovered in Alberta Canada.

Activities:

- You could purchase English muffins and have the participants make their own pizzas. Just provide toppings, cheese, and sauce. Each pizza can represent the moon and sun.

NOVEMBER

History of Cornucopia

Food:
Share a thanksgiving dinner with the group. Have everyone plan the menu, and have each family bring in one of the side dishes, and the center provide the meat. Decorate the center of the table with a cornucopia.

Crafts:
Make placemats for each participant of the meal. Cut out a horn shaped brown cornucopia, and glue it to the center of the placemat. Then cut out fruit, vegetables, and nuts to glue cascading out of the cornucopia.

Use cornucopia pattern at the bottom of this lesson to color. Cut out and glue onto a 17x22 piece of construction paper.

Purchase a cornucopia for each participant. Buy fake fruit, vegetables, nuts and flowers to decorate your own centerpiece for thanksgiving table. Use Styrofoam in the center to attach the fake food and flower items to.

History:
Cornucopias were found in Greek and Roman mythology 3,000 years ago. The name, cornucopia, came from a Latin translation meaning horn of abundance. Some people call cornucopias, horn of plenty. This cone shaped container was filled to overflowing with produce, flowers, and nuts when they are displayed on a Thanksgiving table as the centerpiece.

In Asia and Europe harvesters would fasten a cone-shaped basket around their waist when harvesting the produce from the fields. This gathering basket would allow a wonderful collection container while leaving one's hands free to collect the harvest with two hands.

In Roman mythology, Heracles was noted for ripping the horns off the river god Achelous. As new mythological creatures were developed over time, many dealing with harvest were drawn with a horn feature, resembling the cornucopia. Many of the new gods' depictions of the earth, agriculture, minerals, and spiritual wealth had cornucopia shaped horns.

New versions of the Cornucopia are hollow horn shaped baskets filled to overflowing with fruit, vegetables, nuts, and flowers. This overflowing centerpiece during Thanksgiving holiday, demonstrated the abundance of blessings we have received from our God this harvest season. This display of fruit, vegetables and nuts show how gracious God has been to us. The overflowing cornucopia reminds us of the blessings

God has bestowed on us over the holiday season.

Today cornucopia is solely used for Thanksgiving decorations and centerpiece of your Thanksgiving table. The sense of abundance and bounty are what this display brings to our minds, and ultimately how thankful we are for God's blessings on us during our thanksgiving season.

Activities:

- Use the one cornucopia to color the beautiful display of fruit. Frame it for a decoration, or use the drawing on a Thanksgiving card for your family member or friend.
- Use the cornucopia with the lines to write what you are thankful for in life.

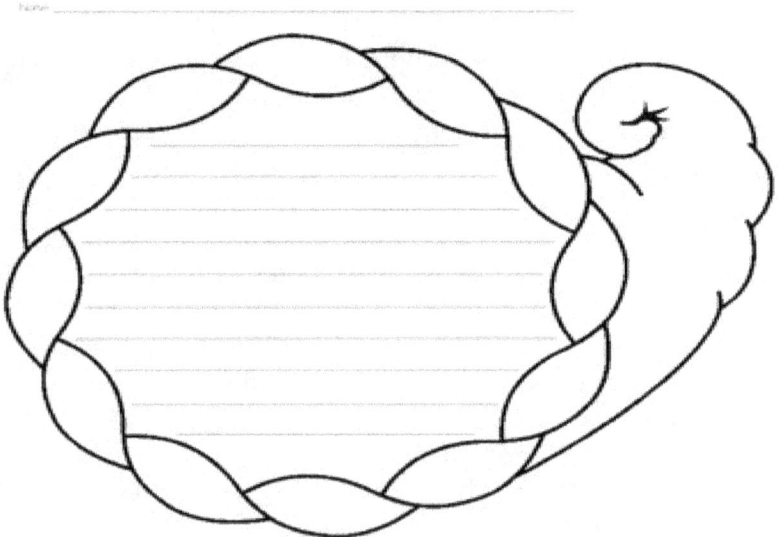

National Black Bear Day

Food:

- Bear Claws. Coffee and tea.

Craft:

- Purchase wooden bear shapes, and black, dark brown, gray, cinnamon, yellowish brown, and white acrylic paints.

- Brown, and gray felt. Poly-fil craft stuffing. Black 1/4-inch buttons, for eyes. Brown thread and sewing needles, craft/sewing pins. White acrylic paint. Cut two of the bears out of the brown felt, (use pattern below). On one side of the bear, sew on the two bear eyes. Next, put the two bear shapes together, making sure the eyes are facing out. Sew the two bear shapes together around the edge, make sure to leave a two-inch opening at the top of the bears head to put the stuffing inside the bear. Make sure you fill the arms and legs first and then the belly and head last. Sew up the top of the head. Take a touch of white paint to give the eyes a little accent color.

History:

The most common bear in North America is the black bear. If you spot a black bear, you might think that their fur is only black, but some are dark brown, cinnamon, or yellow brown. Although their eyes are blue at birth, they turn brown as they age. Their skin around their face and hands is gray.

Brown bears are 4-7 feet long from head to toe, with small eyes, a long cone shaped brown nose, rounded eyes, and short tail. These large animals weigh between 150 to 500 pounds. In New Brunswick, in 1972 the largest black bear caught and killed weighed 902 pounds. This was after it was dressed, prior estimated weighed was 1000 pounds.

So where can you find these beautiful animals? You will find them in the forest areas of USA, Canada, and Mexico. The forests go as far south as Florida, west as Mexico and north to Canada and Alaska. They live in a variety of habitat types that can give them coniferous and deciduous meals. Most of their diet is plant based. Coniferous forests provide evergreen trees that bears can scale to get pine needles, pinecones, and leaves. They also eat herbs, grasses, roots, buds, shoots, honey, nuts, fruit, berries, and seeds. The deciduous forests have dead limbs that provide food as well. Bears also eat fish, small mammals, insects, dead animals, and garbage left by hikers. We know that black bears in Alaska and Northern America eats salmon.

As bears rise in the morning, about a half an hour before sunrise, they are hungry and active. Their day consists of one or two naps during their day and hit the hay about two hours after sunset. When bears are active at night, they are trying to avoid other bears or hunters in the woods. Surprisingly, bears hibernate for months without food, water or going to the bathroom.

Bears travel alone unless they are mating or have baby cubs to attend. Mating season is June and July so that the cubs will be born in January or February. Bears are pregnant for 215 days, about 7 1/2 months. The average litter size is 2-3 cubs, but occasionally mama bears have litters as large as five cubs. The cub's birth weight is about ½ to 1 pound. By fall, cub's weight is from 15 pounds to more than 165 pounds depending on the food supply. Park Rangers estimate black bear population to be 750,000.

Parenting for the cubs lasts for 16-17 months, rarely longer. The mama cubs must mate again in late May or June. Before they mate, they force their year-old cubs to stop traveling with them and branch out on their own. These baby cubs are ready to mate between 2 to 11 years, depending on their ability to find food. Typically, a cub mates between 3 to 7 years.

If the food supply is scarce, cubs will wait for 3-4 years to mate, unless they have the available food to sustain a pregnancy, and then they will be mating at age 2. Mama cub's mate every two years, unless they lose their litter, then they will mate again the following year.

Unfortunately, hunters kill more male black bears, making their ration 1 male to 2-5 female black bears. This is quite a difference than when they are born. The litter's numbers are 50:50 of males to females.

Bears have good vision near and far. Bears approximate vision distance, is over two hundred yards. They also can see colors. Bears hearing is excellent too. They can hear much better than human is hearing. Their top senses are their smell. Black bears mucosa area in their nose is about 100 times larger. The size of their nostrils makes their smell extraordinary. Black bears also have excellent hearing. A small noise like chattering teeth, grunting animals, or human talking can attract their attention.

Black bears are very smart animal. They have large brains and is one of the most intelligent mammals. Bears navigate easily in the woods because they can remember their trails. They are mobile and can run up to 30 miles per hour. Black bears are great swimmers. They swim 1 ½ miles up to 9 miles and do it quickly.

Now that you know the details of the black bear, you might want to start training to run faster than 30 miles per hour if you plan to go hiking in these areas of the woods.

Activities:

• How is Your **Memory Activity?** (see puzzle below) Answer questions as the group on the history of the black bear.

How is Your Memory Activity?

1. What colors are black bears?

2. How big do black bears get?

3. How big do black bears get?

4. Where do the black bears live?

5. What do black bears eat?

6. How long do they hibernate?

7. How many cubs do they have?

8. What months do black bears mate?

9. What month are black bears born?

10. What is the weight of most average black bears?

11. What was the heaviest black bear known?

12. How long does it take black bears to have a baby?

13. What do black bears eat?

14. When do mama bears let their babies leave their mama's?

15. How fast do the black bears run?

16. Do black bears have good sight?

17. How far can they see?

18. Do black bears have good hearing?

19. What sense is the best for black bears?

20. When are black bears most active?

Learning about Northern Cardinals

Food:
- Chex Trail Mix, and Muddy Buddy Mix. (recipes below) These treats will resemble bird feed. Different teas and Coffee

Crafts:
- Cut bird shapes out of cardboard. (see bird body pattern) Use all red, tan, orange, and black yarn. Purchase tan, red, orange bird feathers for the top notch of the bird and side wings. Wrap the red yarn around the bird body and the black around the face of the bird. For female Cardinal, cover the body with a tan body. Use orange feather for the top notch, wings, and part of the tail. Use orange or red markers for their beaks.
- Use clay to mold a cardinal bird. Complete the birds two before the project so it can dry for painting. Or you can mold the birds the day of the activity and paint the birds when they dry another day. You will need black, red, tan, and orange acrylic or tempera paint.

History.

Looking outside at your bird feeder, you see a variety of birds. One of the most favorite bird that you will see feeding at the feeder is the Northern Cardinal. This beautiful bird can be found in southeastern Canada, all the way to eastern United States. Cardinals can be found from Maine to Minnesota, to Texas and all through Mexico, Belize, and Guatemala.

The male Cardinal is a beautiful red bird with a black mask face. His female counter part is subdued, with shades of light brown, with reddish highlights and dark coloration around their eyes and beak. Cardinals are medium size birds that are 8 inches in length.

Seven states have the Northern Cardinal as the state bird. Do you know which states they are? The seven states include Illinois, Indiana, Kentucky, North Carolina, Ohio, Virginia, and West Virginia. This beautiful bird is easy to spot because of its bright red male body and head. These beautiful birds feed on grains, fruit and occasionally insects.

Cardinals do not go south for the winter like some birds, they remain in the Northern states. You can often see them purchased on a tree limb in the winter. Their bright color is a beautiful site to see, especially with the white backdrop of snow. Northern Cardinal males are very territorial during mating season, driving off other males in the area. Cardinals mate with the same female each mating season, and they breed 2 or 3 times each summer. The nests are built by female Cardinals, using shrubs or bushes, to hold their 3-4 eggs clutch. The baby birds have a short incubation period, only 11-13 days. When baby Cardinals are born, they are all tan in color while they are young. As they grow, the females remain tan in color, but the males turn bright red with a black mask face.

After the baby's hatch, both the male and female birds gather food to feed the baby birds. In the beginning the baby birds feed on insects. Both parents continue to feed the babies for several weeks after leaving the nest, until they are mature enough to leave the parents' care. In about ten days, you will see the baby birds begin to learn to fly. The young birds will fly in a group until they are mature enough to find where they want to put down roots. Northern Cardinals live in the wild for about fifteen years until their death.

Some interesting facts about the Northern Cardinal is their red coloring. Cardinals get their bright red color from the pigments found in berries and other plants in their diets. Northern Cardinals males molt in the fall after mating season is over. While they are molting, they are tan in color, but when their feathers grow back, they dawn that beautiful bright red body and black mask face. While molting, Cardinals live in the forest edges and grasslands with lots of shrubbery and thickets, to keep their last clutch of babies hidden and safe.

Although the females Cardinals are chattier than males Cardinals, they are both loud singers to defend their territories. The female Cardinal has a more involved songs, but the male uses his song for a mating call. The sound of the bird songs has been described as; "whoit, whoit," or "wacheer, wacheer." If you hear or see Cardinals in your area, to try to attract then to your bird feeder, try filling the feeder with suet, peanuts, fresh berries and cracked corn. As you look for bird seed, avoid mixed feed with ingredients that has seeds with lots of fillers.

If you have cats or dogs who like to chase birds, you might want to watch for Cardinals safety around them in your yard. Cardinals feed close to the ground, not more than 5 feet above the ground, so make sure to provide a safe place for them to eat and birdbath away from danger. Using a flat dish for bird feed allows the birds to rest while they eat.

Northern Cardinal remain in the North all year round. So, providing a place for them to drink and bath will make it attractive for them to remain in your yard. A heated bird bath in the winter, keeps them enjoying your back yard all year round. Planting evergreen trees and shrubs in your yard, allows for a place for Northern Cardinals to hide from their enemies, some of their favorite shrubs are juniper, honeysuckle, grapevines, and dogwood trees, which also provides the birds to be safe. Other plants that Cardinals enjoy are blueberries, mulberries, or blackberries. Planting berries will ensure Cardinals will visit your yard for meals often.

Activities:
- Make Muddy Buddies and Chex Party Mix

Chex™ Muddy Buddy
18 Servings

This classic chocolate, peanut butter and powdered sugar mix has been a part of families' kitchens for years. An easy snack for kids to make, this quick recipe can be customized for any occasion, transforming Chex™ cereal into a delicious treat in just 15 minutes. We call it Muddy Buddies™, but you may hear it called by different names as a nod to its resemblance to puppy food. We do not blame you, it is doggone good!

Ingredients:
- 9 cups Rice Chex™, Corn Chex™ or Chocolate Chex™ cereal (or combination)
- 1 cup semisweet chocolate chips
- 1/2 cup peanut butter

- 1/4 cup butter or margarine
- 1 teaspoon vanilla
- 1 1/2 cups powdered sugar
-

Preparation

1. Into large bowl, measure cereal; set aside.

2. In 1-quart microwavable bowl, microwave chocolate chips, peanut butter and butter uncovered on High 1 minute; stir. Microwave about 30 seconds longer or until mixture can be stirred smooth. Stir in vanilla. Pour mixture over cereal, stirring until evenly coated. Pour into 2-gallon resealable plastic bag.

Original Chex™ Party Mix
0.5 Servings

It is the time-tested party snack everyone loves—and is ready in just 15 minutes! Win your next gathering by bringing Original Chex Party Mix.

Ingredients:

- 3 cups Corn Chex™ cereal
- 3 cups Rice Chex™ cereal
- 3 cups Wheat Chex™ cereal
- 1 cup mixed nuts
- 1 cup bite-size pretzels
- 1 cup garlic-flavor bite-size bagel chips or regular-size bagel chips, broken into 1-inch pieces
- 6 tablespoons butter or margarine
- 2 tablespoons Worcestershire sauce
- 1 1/2 teaspoons seasoned salt
- 3/4 teaspoon garlic powder
- 1/2 teaspoon onion powder

Preparation:

1. In large microwavable bowl, mix cereals, nuts, pretzels, and bagel chips; set aside. In small microwavable bowl, microwave butter uncovered on High about 40 seconds or until melted. Stir in seasonings. Pour over cereal mixture; stir until evenly coated.

2. Microwave uncovered on High 5 to 6 minutes, thoroughly stirring every 2 minutes. Spread on paper towels to cool. Store in airtight container

3. Tips:

- Substitution: The original recipe includes Corn Chex™, Rice Chex™ and Wheat Chex™. You can mix and match to suit your taste—just use a total of 9 cups of cereal.

- Healthy: To reduce the fat to 2 grams and the calories to 80 per serving, use 3 tablespoons margarine instead of the 6 tablespoons butter, omit mixed nuts and use fat-free bagel chips.

- Presentation/Garnish: Make enough of this favorite mix to package up as gifts for special friends—it is so good and always a welcome surprise!

- Pre-heat oven to 250°. Put cereal and seasoning mixture into ungreased roasting pan and bake for 1 hour, stirring every 15 minutes. Spread on paper towels to cool, about 15 minutes.

DECEMBER

Favorite Toys as a Child

Food:

- Old fashioned candy. Moon Pies, Ice cream sodas or Coke or Root Beer Floats.

Crafts:

- Folded Cooties catcher out of paper. Take a square piece of paper, fold all the corners to the center so that the points meet. Turn the folded paper over so that these folds are on the table. Next turn up these corners to meet in the center, like you did on the first side. Then fold the paper in half, unfold and fold the other side in half. Lift the flaps on the first folded side to stick your fingers into them so you can move your fingers open and shut making the paper open and shut with your fingers. After you know that you Cootie works, open each of the 8 flaps and put a fortune under each flap. On the outside of the flaps that you have your fingers in, write numbers. When you are finished making your Cootie Catcher or Fortune teller, ask someone to pick a number. Whatever the number is, you spell it as you open and shut your fingers, repeat this process 2-3 times and then open the last number they chose and read them their fortune.

- Make an old-time toy. Get 2 large buttons and string. Cut a 36-inch length of string. Lace the string into one hole in the bottom and then out of the other hole of the same button. Take the other end of the string and do the same with the other button and tie the string together. Put the buttons in the center of the string an put each end of the string around each of your index fingers. Swing the buttons in the center so that they twist around each other. When twisted together, begin to pull backwards on your index fingers and see the buttons spin around. The buttons will make a humming noise as they spin around. Old fashioned toy.

History:

As we think back to our childhood memories our mind returns to the many toys we enjoyed playing with as we were growing up. One of the earliest toys that our parents would entertain us with was bubbles. Sitting over a pan of soapy water playing in the water and blowing bubbles. It was not until 1940 that bottle bubbles became packaged in Chicago by a cleaning-supply company allowing bubbles to be carried to parks and picnics for entertaining the children. Now millions of bottles of bubbles are sold with wands to create a variety of sizes of bubbles.

Another popular toy child enjoyed were Yo-yos. This round toy on a string allowed children to spend hours trying to perfect tricks like, walking the dog, around the corner, skin the cat, and rock the baby, to name a few.

If you wanted to play on the floor you might see children spinning a top, playing jacks, or shooting marbles. Competition for who can shoot the best marbles or capture the most jacks in one hand without missing to catch the ball was the winner. Children also enjoyed watching the top spin for hours while they tried to spin it faster and longer the next time.

Jump ropes, skates, and balls were a staple for children's summertime play. These simple toys provided hours of fun for children in the neighborhood play. Another fun wooden toy was the paddle ball. This wooden paddle with a ball attached with an elastic string was good for coordination and skill development. The only problem was when the ball can off, and our parents used it as a discipline paddle. Boys enjoyed many wooden toys such as slingshots, toy trains, and trucks.

Many children enjoyed a new toy developed by Richard T. James in 1943 and demonstrated at Gimbel's department store in Philadelphia in November that year for Christmas. Board games were another fun toy that children could play with their parents. Some of those included checkers, chess, and Parcheesi.

Think back, what was your favorite game as a child?

Activities:

- Play with some of the old toys like yo-yo's, tiddlywinks, jacks, slinky or paddles with ball attached.
- You can have a contest to see who can keep the paddle ball going the longest.
- Word Search Favorite Childhood Toys Puzzle

FAVORITE CHILDHOOD TOYS
WORD SEARCH

```
K Y P G J S G K J L R S D S Z
M E T O N A I N L A R K O Y R
N S E Q G C C A O Y H N D S I
M N D S K O B K K P H I G E F
B F R B O E S N S U H W E L Z
G Q A M L G I T L V C Y B B K
B L J D R L D L I Z P L A R E
L V D D S E E N M C X D L A G
H A G M H D P Z A S K D L M K
P L L A B T F O S E T I N C P
J Y O Y O S J T R C D T O U T
X V B P S Y P U D P X I Z W A
H O P S C O T C H L M P H V G
L K Y D M K Q E J Z K U R Q C
P R B Z V M J W T D L X J I W
```

DODGE BALL	HIDE-AND-GO-SEEK	HOP SCOTCH
JACKS	JUMP ROPE	KICK BALL
MARBLES	PADDLE BALL	POGO STICK
SLINKY	SOFT BALL	TAG
TIDDLY WINKS	YOYOS	

National Eggnog Day

Food:

• Eggnog, Christmas cookies, fruitcake.

Craft:

• Purchase cardboard craft eggs. They can be purchased at hobby stores, or Oriental Trading Company. Purchase acrylic paint in different colors, narrow ribbons for hangers. Make a hole in the top of the egg and tie a narrow ribbon Paint designs on the eggs.

• Using the same cardboard eggs, take half of the eggs, and paint the outer and inner parts of the egg, let them dry. Using decorative braid to decorate the edges of the opening of each side of the egg's halves. Get small items to decorate inside each egg. Attach narrow ribbon on the tops of eggs to hang them on the tree. Or get plastic circles from the sewing department to glue on the bottom to set the eggs up so the scenes can be enjoyed.

History:

A 19th century, a mixture of sugar, milk, eggs, brandy, and rum, became a popular drink, called eggnog. The origin of eggnog was in East Anglia, England. The name began as Egg Flip, but the English Colonies used the term "grog, for drinks including rum. The name gradually changed to "egg-and-grog," and later shortened to eggnog.

The word "nog," originated in 1693, from the carved mugs that the brandy was served out of in East Anglia. Refrigeration was scarce in London, so drinks with milk were rare and expensive, so the wealthy were more likely to have eggnog originally, that is why brandy, Nadeira or sherry were added. In 1775, a Maryland clergyman, Jonathan Boucher, wrote a poem about this drink, but the poem was not published until 30 years after his death.

Eggnog, moved across the Atlantic Ocean in the 1765 - 1775, because of the tax on brandy and wines. Inexpensive liquors were found in the Caribbean, so trade began as a more affordable way to have eggnog drinks during the holidays. The growth of cattle farms producing milk, helped to advance this drink. Another change was during the Revolutionary War, when prices of liquor dropped, allowing more eggnog drinkers. Domestic whiskey began being used as well, and bourbon was found in the eggnog mixtures. New-Jersey Journal of March 26, 1788,

New-Jersey Journal, wrote an article about a man enjoying a wonderful new drink, eggnog, in their March 1788 edition. This article got readers curious to taste this new holiday drink. It was not until 1869 that Webster's Dictionary, shared and defined the word "eggnog," in the revised printing.

Debates still go on about where eggnog, originated, some say this was an early medieval British drink. Some hot drinks with milk and wine or ale were home remedies. They tasted good, so they started drinking them for pleasure too. Spices were added for a festive tasting drink on a cold day. Monks were even known to indulge in this popular drink in the 13th century. In the Victorian Era, gin was the alcohol used in eggnog drinks.

Records show the even President's served eggnog. George Washington, the first President, served eggnog with rye whiskey, rum, or sherry to his visitors. His recipe was 1 quart of cream, 1 quart of milk, 1 dozen eggs, 12 tablespoons of sugar, 1 pint of brandy, 1/2-pint rye whiskey, 1/2 Jamaica rum, and 1/4 pint of sherry. The yokes were beaten before adding them, with all the other ingredients. Egg whites were mixed separated and whipped up stiff, before adding to mixture at the end. The mixture sat for several days to let the flavors marry for better taste, before serving it to guests.

On some menu's, you find a "Tome and Jerry," drink. This is a form of eggnog, invented by Pierce Egan in 1820's. Traditionally, it is served at Christmastime, in a mug with brandy. United States serve this style eggnog in some English restaurants. If you travel to Canada, you will find eggnog drinks around the holidays too. Puerto Rico serves an eggnog, with rum and coconut juice or coconut milk instead of cream.

Mexico changes the drink by adding cinnamon and rum, while Peru uses beer instead of rum or wine. Germany's 1904 version has eggs, lemon juice, sugar, white wine, and rum, but Iceland, serves the eggnog hot as a dessert to finish off your meal.

Although there are a variety of ways to serve your eggnog, not everyone likes to enjoy this drink during the holidays. It is like fruitcake, you either love eggnog or you hate it, regardless you will see people enjoying this festive drink during the holiday times.

Activities:

• Sing the 12 Days of Christmas, to see who can remember all the gifts in the song.

• Sing Christmas carols.

History of Ugly Christmas Sweaters

Food:

● Christmas cookies, hot chocolate, and mulled cider.

Crafts:

● Have the participants bring an old sweater that they are not wearing to decorate. Purchase pom-poms, stars, buttons, Christmas felt Santa's, reindeer, snowman, Christmas balls etc., any decorations that can be used that you find.

● Get difference colors of felt, and cut them out into sweater shapes, using the pattern below. Get different holiday designs in felt, pom poms, ribbons, buttons, or anything that would decorate a small felt sweater. Then put a ribbon or yarn on the top and use it as an ornament.

History:

In the 1950's when Christmas started becoming commercialized, Christmas sweater started becoming popular. Teachers adorned a Christmas sweater with blinking lights, or with a Santa with a furry beard to celebrate the holidays for their classes. You might see entire families wearing the same style Christmas sweater, starting with the dad, and ending with the smallest child.

Christmas sweaters did not get started as a trend until the 1980's. "Jingle bell" sweaters was how they were advertisers. As the popularity grew, Christmas sweaters became more and more elaborate and sometimes gaudy. As more people started wearing Christmas sweaters, people tried to top the next person's sweater, with the most outlandish style.

In the 1990's was the birth of the Ugly Sweater Christmas parties. These parties started in Vancouver, Canada. Soon the Ugly Sweater parties spread to the United States, many times having themes for these parties.

Invitations to Ugly Sweater parties, leads people to yard sales and consignment shops to find ugly Christmas sweaters cheap. You cannot wear the same sweater year after year, so the search for the perfect new sweater is a must.

Fun Ugly Sweater parties were still going strong in the 2010, so fashion designers decided to capitalize on this money maker by new designs. Some were retro designs, like holly wreaths and Christmas bells, while others were wild Christmas trees with blinking lights or reindeer with blinking red nose.

Christmas movies, like National Lampoon's Christmas Vacation, showed Chevy Chase sporting all kinds of gaudy Christmas sweaters. This movie was first released in 1983, but had subsequent releases in 1986, 1991, 1995 and 1999. The movies was also released for purchase in DVD in 1997. Because of the many releases, and the home DVD, many generations were wearing the ugly Christmas sweaters, and the parties were seen by all age groups.

If you want to brighten up your holiday season, try wearing one of these fun creations, or better yet, host an Ugly Sweater party and see what fun you can enjoy with family and friends.

Activities:

● Seek a word puzzle.

● Adjectives that describes an ugly sweater, or an Ugly Sweater party. Write "Ugly Sweater Party, down the white board or on a piece of paper and discipline the sweaters or parties. U = unique, G = great, L -= lavish, Y= Yummy food etc.

UGLY SWEATER PATTERN

National Candy Cane Day – December 26

Food:

- Hot cocoa with a candy cane in it. Candy cane shaped cookies.
- Peppermint brittle and cocoa, coffee, and peppermint tea.
- Tea party with peppermint cocoa, peppermint tea, tea sandwiches.

Crafts:

- Get pipe cleaners, and red and white plastic beads. Thread the red and white beads onto the pipe cleaner, alternating the colors. When you finish getting the pipe cleaner full, turn the pipe cleaner under to keep the beads on the pipe cleaner. Then make the pipe cleaner hook to hang on your tree. You can make one each or more.
- Use real candy canes, put small google eyes on the curved part, on the top curve use a brown pipe cleaner to make antlers, and then use a small red pom-pom for Rudolph's nose.
- Candy Cane Star

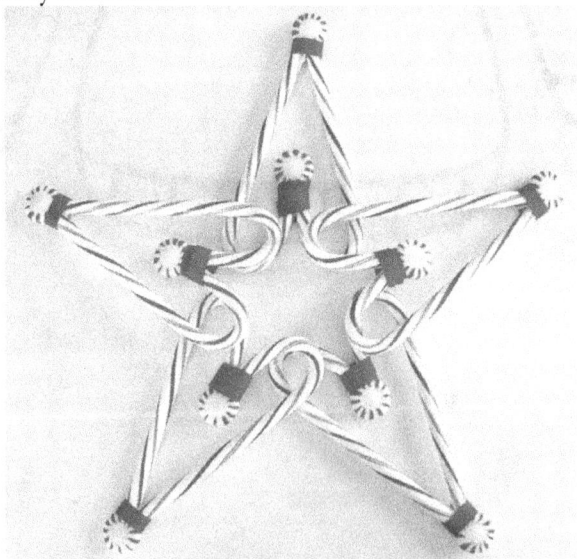

History:

In the 17th century, Germany introduced a sweet, red, and white shepherd hook shaped treat to children to enjoy at the holidays. Candy canes originated in 1670 when a choir director of church children, gave this crooked top treat to the children after the Christmas performance. The candy cane shape resembling the Christian Bishops crosier and was resemblance of the Good Shepherd Jesus.

Red and white candy canes found during the holidays to give as a little treat from Santa, at parties or to decorate one's Christmas tree. But where did this peppermint treat come from? In 1844, the first peppermint candy was a red and white stick without a curved top. It was not until the 1866; peppermint stick was molded into a crook and hung on the Christmas tree for children, and friends who might visit during the holidays.

A few fun facts about the candy cane are that it averages about five inches tall. This holiday treat is not sugar or calorie free, it does not have any cholesterol or fat for the consumers. The first candy canes were made by hand, but in 1921 Brasher O. Waterfield invented the first candy cane making machine.

Bob McCormack and his brother-in-law, Gregory Keller decided this sugary treat would be a great treat for their family and friends, so they began producing them to distribute. Seeing how many people really enjoyed this peppermint cane, they decided to make a machine to mass produce them for a larger consumer to enjoy. Originally the treat was only found in peppermint, but today there are a variety of colors and flavors produced around the holiday for treats and gift giving.

The first Candy Cane world record was 51 feet long, made by Alain Roby from Geneva, but candy maker Sensei Bob Gay passed this record in New York, New York and it measured 8.08 feet long.

In 1847, all-white candy canes were in the United States, the peppermint sticks enjoyed so much in Germany and Sweden, that German-Swedish immigrants brought the treat with them when they came to America. The all-white candy stick remained all white until the 1900s when the red stripes were added for St. Nicholas to handout for Christmas.

Each year candy canes are the top selling candy between Thanksgiving and Christmas, with sales reaching 1.76 billion. The second week of December is when the sales take off, probably because people decorated their tree, give them to friends and enjoy snacking on them during the holiday season.

Has talking about candy canes have made you want one? Dig into this refreshing treat; it only has 55 calories for this five-inch stick. Carry them with you as you go around during the holiday to brighten the faces of children and friends that you meet throughout this busy season of the year.

Activities

- **Read the *Legend of the Candy Cane:***

The Legend of the Candy Cane

Many years ago, a candy maker wanted to make a candy at Christmas time that would serve as a witness to his Christian faith. He wanted to incorporate several symbols for the birth, ministry and death of Jesus. He began with a stick of pure white hard candy; white to symbolize the Virgin Birth and the sinless nature of Jesus; hard to symbolize the solid rock, the foundation of the Church; firmness to represent the promise of God.

The candymaker made the candy in the form of a "J" to represent the name of Jesus, who came to earth as our Savior. He thought it could also represent the staff of the Good Shepherd, with which he reached down into the ditches of the world to lift out the fallen lambs who, like all sheep, have gone astray.

Thinking that the candy was somewhat plain, the candymaker stained it with red stripes. He used three small stripes to show the stripes of the scourging Jesus received, by which we are healed. The large red stripe was for the blood shed by Christ on the cross so that we could have the promise of eternal life. Unfortunately, the candy became known as a candy cane - a meaningless decoration seen at Christmas time. But the true meaning is still there for those who have eyes to see and ears to hear.

https://www.google.com/search?q=legend+of+the+Candy+CAne&rls=com.microsoft:en-US:IE-Address&sxsrf=ALeKk02-M0vtLji9MZfaouwe2pRdrv0R1g:1606923686635&tbm=isch&source=iu&ictx=1&fir=OioQ-6-87K5owM%252CpWpY3Jf4SIYjyM%252C_&vet=1&usg=AI4_-kTCSO8OYfqxJTQHr6Qywdu9-hniGQ&sa=X&ved=2ahUKEwiZ-pac0a_tAhVrEFkFHeOBCskQ9QF6BAgPEAE&biw=1093&bih=502#imgrc=OioQ-6-87K5owM

Answer Page

FRUITCAKE INGREDIENTS PUZZLE - from page 6

```
T  S  G  G  E              F                 R
U  S              L              E
N  E        F  R  U  I  T        O  T  S
O  L        N                    T  U
C  F  A  L  L  I  N  A  V  U  G     R
O  R              S  C  B  A
C  I              A  I  R
   S           N  S     A
   I     D  L        T     R
   N  I     E              U
   G  E     M              N
   D        O
            N
```

BUTTER   CANDIED   COCONUT
EGGS   FLOUR   FRUIT
LEMON   NUTS   RAISINS
SELFRISING   SUGAR   VANILLA

BIRDS AROUND THE WORLD PUZZLE - from page 9

```
H           H  C        F              L        B  K
   U  A     A        I           L        L     C
   W  M     R           N  U     U              O
K        M  D           G  C  E                 C
            I     E  A        B  H              A
            N  N  E  E  I                       E
            A  S  G  R  D                       P
            L     D  B     A
         E  S  S  D  R  I  B  K  C  A  L  B
         A              R     C
P  I  G  E  O  N              D     I
         L                 S     H
         E                          C
   L  W  O
```

BLACKBIRD   BLUEBIRDS   CARDINALS
CHICKADEE   EAGLE   FINCH
HAWK   HUMMINGBIRDS   OWL
PEACOCK   PIGEON   SEAGULL

MR. ROGERS NEIGHBORHOOD PUZZLE - from page 32

```
                T   S   Y                       Y
A               R       A           D           D
    T           E   E   O       D               E
        T       V   L   G       L       I       E
            E   I   E       O       L       R   P
            L   I       R       M       E       F
        E   N       R       R       C       Y
    D   A           N       M       F       K       S
    D                       E                   I   T
T   I   G   E   R           H   E               R   N
D   L   I   H   C   R   I   A   F   L       I           G
                                    Y   P
                                    E   L   T   S   A   C
                            D
P   U   S   S   Y   C   A   T
```

CASTLE DANIEL DELIVERY
FAIRCHILD FRIDAY HENRIETTA
KING MCFEELY MRROGERS
PUSSYCAT SPEEDY STRIPED
TIGER TROLLEY

HISTORY OF QUILT NAMES PUZZLE - from page 40

```
            R       G               N       P   S
    C       A   A   R           O       A       I
    I       T   T       A   G       T       T   M
    R       S       S   A   N   C       R       P
    C       H       X   E   H   N   A           L
    L       G       E   W   N   D   Y           I
    E       I   H   O       E   O               C
    F       H   R               L               I
        L   K   S   D   N   I   W                T
            A   E   U   G   A   E   L   Y   V   I Y
            H
S   Q   U   A   R   E
```

CIRCLE GRANNY HALF
HEXAGON HIGHSTAR IVY LEAGUE
LONESTAR PATCHWORK SIMPLICITY
SQUARE TRADE WINDS

SOCK HOP WORDS PUZZLE - from page 59

```
S          R          O                              K
B    R            O                              N
O       E         C                        I
B          G         K                P
B             R         A          D                S
Y                U          N                E    P
C   S   P   E   N   N   Y   B   A   S   D       I   O
P   O   O   D   L   E   S   K   I   R   T   R   N
    C   K               C           E   F   Y   O
    K       E       A               F   T               L
    S               L                   A                   L
            B                   I   O
                    L           O
                S   M   A   E   R   C   E   C   I
```

BLACK AND PINK BOBBY SOCKS BURGERS
COKE FRIES ICE CREAM
LOAFERS PENNY PONYTAILS
POODLE SKIRT ROCK AND ROLL

HISTORY OF KERMIT AND FRIENDS PUZZLE- from page 63

```
                A               E   S   R   O   R
K   E   R   M   I   T   N   A   S   E       Z   E
    A   D               G   I   T               N   K
T   O               L       O   M               O   A
    G           E       O           A       G   E
                C                       L       R   W
                S               F               B   A
                                    R               L
                W   E   D   Y   E   N   O   H       T
Y   G   G   I   P   C   H   E   F               D   E
B       O                                   L       R
    E       Z                                       A
        A       Z   I                                   W
            R       R
```

ANIMAL BEAR BREAKER
CHEF DOG EAGLE
GONZO HONEYDEW KERMIT
MISS PIGGY RAT
RIZZO SCOOTER WALDORF
WALTER

DRIVE-IN MOVIES WORD SCRAMBLE PUZZLE - from page 74

GONE WITH THE WIND

SINGING IN THE RAIN

MY FAIR LADY

IT'S A WONDERFUL LIFE

SCROOGE

MARY POPPINS

GREASE

VIVA LAS VEGAS

OKLAHOMA

WEST SIDE STORY

THE BIRDS

WHITE CHRISTMAS

HIDDEN PUZZLE SOLUTION: DRIVE-IN MOVIES ARE FUN

WAFFFLE TOPPINGS PUZZLE- from page 82

```
S           P       C       E       W   C
  E   E   I       U   A       T       H   C   H
      I   Q   C   R   R   A       I       H   O
      R   A   E   L   Y   P       Y   E   C   Y
      M   R   O   C   I   S   E       R   O   R
  E       C   E   C   R   N           R   L   R
  L       O       E   B   O   E       I   A   E
  H           C       H   E   W   A   E   T   B
C           R               U       S   E   W
  E                           L       C   A   E
  A                               B   H   R   L
M   S   P   R   I   N   K   L   E   S       I   T   P
R   E   T   T   U   B   T   U   N   A   E   P   P   S   A
A   N   A   N   A   B                       S       M
```

BANANA   BLUEBERRIES   CARAMEL
CHERRIES   CHOCOLATE   CHOCOLATE CHIPS
HONEY   ICECREAM   MAPLE
PEANUT BUTTER   SPRINKLES   STRAWBERRY
SYRUP   WHIPPED CREAM

Watchmakers Number Puzzle - from page 91

				16
5	6	5	3	19
6	1	5	1	13
6	3	4	5	18
5	4	2	5	16
22	14	16	14	15

TOMB OF THE UNKNOWN SOLDIERS PUZZLE- from page 96

```
                        S               B    S           V
                    E               U    P           I
C    E    M    E    T    E    R    Y    V    G    N         A           R
S    R    E    I    D    L    O    S    L         E         T           G
     E                        E    N    W    L                          I
B         N                   O         H    L    G                     N
     M         T    E    T              I    A                          I
          O         I    G    U    S         T    F                     A
               T    N    N    K    W    R    E    A    T    H
               I    K    C    E              I    R    O    N    O    H
          L    N    I              L              F
     R    O    L                             F
A    W    C                                       L
N                                                      E
```

ARLINGTON
CLICKS
HONOR
SOLDIER
UNKNOWN
WREATH

BUGLE
FALLEN
RIFFLE
TAPS
VIRGINIA

CEMETERY
GLOVES
SENTINEL
TOMB
WHITE

223

DISCOVERING ALASKA PUZZLE - from page 99

```
N     M              S  T  A  D              A
   R     O        S        H  U  O        L
M  E        O  E              G  R  G        A
   U     H     N  S              I  O     S
   S     K  T     E        L  R  K  D  E  L     S
   R     H     R              Y  A              R
   A        E     O        A  S              A
D        S        R     N     D        E        G
               T              B              O
E  G  A  R  O  H  C  N  A              L
   H  U  S  K  Y  G                 D
G  L  A  C  I  E  R  I  Y
                           L
```

ALASKA	ANCHORAGE	AURORAS
BEARS	DARKNESS	DAYLIGHT
DOGS	GLACIER	GOLD
HUSKY	LIGHTS	MOOSE
MUSHERS	NORTHERN	SLED

COUNTRIES WHO MAKE COFFEE PUZZLE - from page 104

```
      M     C  A     Y           I     A
      A     O     I     R        N     I
      N     S        P     O  D     N
      T     T           O  O  V  R
      E     A           N  I  O  I
G     I     R        E     F  H
   U  V  U  I  M  S     I        T
T  H  A  T  C  I  E  L     I        E
U  C     T  A  Y  X  I  B  R  A  Z  I  L
R  T     E  C     A  I
K  U     M  A  M  W        C
E  D  E  B     A  A  I  B  M  O  L  O  C
Y  N  U     H        L  A  Y  N  E  K
   C  A  E                 A
P  U  E  R  T  O  R  I  C  O
```

BRAZIL	CALIFORNIA	COLOMBIA
COSTARICA	CUBA	DUTCH
ETHIOPIA	GUATEMALA	HAWAII
INDONESIA	IVORY	KENYA
MEXICO	PUERTORICO	TURKEY
VIETNAM	YEMEN	

224

```
B   G   N   I   T   I   C   E   R   M       S   S   H
    L       K           E           R   S   C   C
S       A       L           M       E       O   I   N
    T       C       A   O       H       A   T   E   U
        N       K   R   H   C           R   L   N   L
W           E   I   B   A   C           I   L   C
    R       Z   D   E   O               T   A   E   R
        I       T   U       A           H   B   E
    N       T       T       R       M   C
G           I           S           D   E               S
R   E   A   D   I   N   G       S   T           M
J   A   C   K   S       G       S   I       E
E   L   P   P   A                   C   O   T
                                    P       A
                                            G
```

APPLE	ARITHMETIC	BALL TOSS
BLACK BOARD	CHALK	JACKS
LUNCH	MEMORIZING	POEMS
READING	RECESS	RECITING
SCIENCE	STUDENTS	TAG
TEACHER	WRITING	

FIREFIGHTER'S WORD JUMBLE - from page 133

Answers:

Firefighter

Hose

Dalmatian

Axe

Boots

Oxygen

Mask

Ladder

```
            T   A   C   K   C   A   L   B           R
        E                                   E       K
B   R   O   K   E   N   M   I   R   R   O   R   D   L   N
S                       O                   D   L   F   O
    T                           B               A   E   I   C
        E                               H   L   P   N       K
            P                           R   S   D           O
                O                   E           A   I       N
                    N   D           P                   W   W
                    N   C   E                               O
                        U       N   R                       O
                    K       N       R                       D
                L           Y                   A           D
            A                               C
W   S   A   L   T   T   O   O   F   T   I   B   B   A   R
```

BLACK CAT   BROKEN MIRROR   SALT
FIND A PENNY   KNOCK ON WOOD   RABBIT FOOT
WALK UNDER LADDER   SPELL   STEP ON CRACK
    WISHBONE

Favorite Childhood Toys Word Search Puzzle - from page 153

```
K       P       J           K       L       S   D
    E       O       A   I       L       K   O
        E       G   C   C       A       Y       N   D   S
            S   K   O   B   K   K           I   G   E
            B   O   E   S   N   S           W   E   L
        A       L   G   I   T               Y   B   B
    L       D       L   D       I           L   A   R
L       D       S   E   E   N       C       D   L   A
    A               P       A       K   D   L   M
P   L   L   A   B   T   F   O   S   E       I
    Y   O   Y   O   S   S       R       D   T           T
                            P               I           A
H   O   P   S   C   O   T   C   H       M       H       G
                                    U
                                        J
```

DODGE BALL   **HIDE-AND-GO-SEEK**   **HOP SCOTCH**
JACKS   **JUMP ROPE**   **KICK BALL**
MARBLES   **PADDLE BALL**   **POGO STICK**
SLINKY   **SOFT BALL**   **TAG**

TIDDLY WINKS   **YOYOS**

www.ingramcontent.com/pod-product-compliance
Lightning Source LLC
Chambersburg PA
CBHW070412270326
41926CB00014B/2790